CONTEMPORARY SCOTTISH POETRY

CONTEMPORARY
SCOTTISH POETRY

INDIVIDUALS AND CONTEXTS

ROBIN FULTON

MACDONALD PUBLISHERS
Loanhead · Midlothian
1974

Published by
Macdonald Publishers
Edgefield Road, Loanhead, Midlothian

Printed by
Macdonald Printers, (Edinburgh) Limited
Edgefield Road, Loanhead, Midlothian

With the support of the Scottish Arts Council

CHURCH AND RECTORY AT BATOCHE

MASS GRAVE — BATOCHE

Preface

In the last two decades or so, and particularly in the sixties, Scottish poets have been very productive. The quantity and variety of their work however has not been matched by a corresponding critical activity. Granted, at regular intervals various magazines publish surveys and in so far as these are informative they are useful but in so far as they attempt to be evaluative the circumstances restrict comment to cryptic thumb-nail judgments; indeed in some instances what we have are mere thumbs-up-or-thumbs-down verdicts. And of course the customary reviewing business has dealt with most collections produced, though there have been some surprising omissions in this area, not only in the English but also in the Scottish press. Here too circumstances are restricting. There is no reason why useful critical pointers should not be made in the narrow confines of a review—they often are—but with disappointing frequency the predictable adjectives and the unsupported generalisations recur. What has been lacking, as an essential background both to the reviewing of new work and to the evolution of wider viewpoints, is basic critical spadework such as description, analysis and comparison. So while all the poets discussed here "need no introduction," as the chairmen say, that in another sense is where criticism must begin.

That this book does not attempt a comprehensive survey should be obvious from the fact that of the fifty-one poets represented in MacCaig and Scott's *Contemporary Scottish Verse 1959-1969* (Calder, 1970), thirty-two are not discussed here. What I have done is first to select three poets—Edwin Morgan, Iain Crichton Smith and Norman MacCaig—whose work certainly owes a great deal to local geographical and social contexts but is substantial and individual enough to defy the enclosing implications of any such defined contexts. Then I grouped various other poets whose work, while markedly individual, can, for undogmatic purposes of discussion, be usefully considered in terms of such contexts. In Chapter Four we have poetry which owes much of its motivation to a strong sense of belonging to a geographical and social locality—George Bruce,

Derick Thomson, George Mackay Brown, Stewart Conn and Roderick Watson. In Chapter Five we have poetry which owes more to the motivation of personal psychological pressures— W. S. Graham, Kenneth White, David Black, Alan Jackson and Alasdair Maclean. Local loyalties in the work of these poets may be shifting or insignificant, though in Alasdair Maclean we have an interesting link between the two contexts. Finally, a different kind of context—the linguistic one: Chapter Six considers the present position of non-English writing and pays particular attention to the work of Robert Garioch.

The poets here to whom I respond most positively have all been represented—some of them substantially—in *Lines Review*. Indeed my interest in their poetry developed in the course of practical editorial work and it is appropriate to acknowledge the close connection between this book and the magazine. The book can perhaps be regarded as an extended editorial, confirming the preferences and assumptions already demonstrated in practice over the past seven or eight years.

Contents

INDIVIDUALS

I

EDWIN MORGAN

MacDiarmid's plea, as stated repeatedly in his critical writings and illustrated voluminously in his poetry, for a literature whose attitude towards the contemporary world is inclusive rather than exclusive, is subjected to the same dialectical contrariness as are all his major themes. On the one hand it has not prevented his supporting work (by young writers for instance) whose attitudes are narrow; on the other he has not deemed it incompatible with an elitism that would out-Leavis Leavis. For every gesture in one direction there is at least one equally vigorous gesture in the opposite direction, so while we may expect MacDiarmid to recognise and welcome the wide range and openness of Morgan's work as a refreshing element in contemporary Scottish poetry, this is not necessarily the case. Granted, the temperamental differences are considerable. MacDiarmid is a predator: with the enthusiasm and frequent inaccuracy of a voracious autodidact he has rifled world literature, history and science for material which can be absorbed into his own prevailing concerns. The movement is inwards, and fidelity to the sources is not highly regarded. With Morgan, the movement is outwards, and in his translation and criticism fidelity towards and respect for the sources is paramount. Thus there is little excuse for doubt about MacDiarmid's intentions: indeed, in certain phases, such as *The Kind of Poetry I Want*, there is a serious question as to the extent to which the programme has supplanted the poetry. In Morgan's case, a central line through his poetry is more difficult to determine, and he has admitted to this difficulty on his own part.[1]

However there is one possible line which will serve to relate his most important work coherently and that is best described in terms of the poem "Floating off to Timor"[2]. It postulates an unresolved tension between a romantic desire for exotic distances and a particular human concern for local unromantic circumstances. The relative passivity of the romantic desire is signalled in the title, "floating" suggesting ease and drifting whereas "sailing" would have been active and positive. The first two lines

If only we'd been strangers
we'd be floating off to Timor

suggest both the longing for this kind of escape ("if only") and the recognition that its fulfilment is illusory, depending on a blindness towards reality ("strangers"). The precise location and circumstances of such a dream-voyage are inevitably hazy.

> But here we are care
> of the black roofs.

Home, actuality, the familiar and defined (for all that our belonging may be c/o, as with lodgers) has an exact time and place and is grimy. Given the fact of shipbuilding in an industrial city, where the cranes share the skyline with pseudo-gothic spires and high-rise flats and the new hulls rise above the crumbling tenements, such a tension of desires is perhaps inevitable.

> It's living with ships
> makes a rough springtime
> and what heart is safe
> when they sing and blow
> their music—they seem
> to swing at some light rope
> like those desires
> we keep for strangers.

The dream may well sully in the home terrain. No doubt wakefulness is healthier. Yet if we are caught in the mesh of local circumstances, we are equally caught in the less tangible mesh of our desires for other circumstances:

> We take in
> the dream, a cloth from the line
> the trains fling sparks on
> in our city. We're better awake.
> But you know I'd take
> you all the same,
> if you were my next stranger.

I suggest then that we can see Morgan's work with a reasonable coherence if we keep in mind this tension between (i) a romantic outgoing urge, indulged with a knowledge of its unfulfillable nature, and (ii) a close local scrutiny of home ground, conducted with a realisation that there are possibilities of life and interest on a much wider scale and in very different circumstances.

14

II

Before following this line through his own poetry it would be
as well here to indicate the extent of Morgan's work as a translator
and to suggest that his ability to tune in to widely differing wave-
lengths is an important contributory factor to the agile wide-ranging
and forward-looking nature of much of his work. He has translated
poetry from, at least, Ancient Greek, Old English, modern Italian,
Spanish, French, German, Russian and Hungarian.[3] A characteristic exercise, printed in *Akros* No. 9 (January 1969), was a study of
three poems about Brooklyn Bridge, by Hart Crane, Mayakovsky
and Lorca; this was followed by translations of Mayakovsky's
Russian into Scots and of Lorca's Spanish into English. Much of
the poetry he has translated has been by poets whose involvement
with social and political issues has been pronounced: Neruda,
Lorca, Brecht, Mayakovsky, Voznesensky (Montale being somewhat of an exception). This has in part been a deliberate attempt to
indicate directions in which post-war British poetry has been reluctant
to extend itself; but in part too it is clearly related to his own poetry
and his desire that it should be accessible and relevant to a broad
range of readership. The linguistic challenge of translating poetry
of virtuosic skill is also highly attractive, particularly, as in Mayakovsky and Voznesensky, when the verbal fireworks are combined with
the projection of a public stance. His use of Scots to translate
Mayakovsky is an interesting example of the possibilities still
available in Scots for providing a more adequate parallel to the
vigorous inventive kind of language used by Mayakovsky than is
available in modern English.[4] His translations of Voznesensky,
on the other hand, are in English and in their inventive parallels
to the word-play of the original they are superior to many of the
more available versions.[5] Morgan's attraction to Weöres is
interesting for other reasons: unlike many of the poets mentioned
Weöres has pursued a resolutely apolitical vocation and while in
his native context this makes him appear as a lonely figure it has
also enabled him to survive several difficult decades. Yet his plurality
of styles, his verbal playfulness, his many masks are clearly features
which offer not only a congenial technical challenge to Morgan
but also a pattern of versatility which has affinities with his own
work.[6]

15

The preface to *Sovpoems* (1961—and long out of print) will illustrate the more polemical aspects of his work as a translator and will also show how these influence his general view of the function of poetry. This small book contained translations from Pasternak (4 poems), Tsvetayeva (1), Mayakovsky (3), Tikhonov (1), Brecht (7), Neruda (3), Martynov (3) and Yevtushenko (2). They were issued with "the desire to redress a balance—to open the door slightly on a world which political (and in part linguistic) considerations have kept too remote from Western writers and readers— to show, if not throw, a few of the lifelines that have been preserved within the European tradition: lifelines which are now as perilous to refuse as they have usually been thought naïve to accept." Referring to the technical liberation of verse from a tired tradition, at the beginning of the modern period, he then tosses a challenge to the modern English tradition: "It is in the different uses made of this liberation that the crucial split between two worlds can be seen emerging. Symbolism, futurism, imagism, and surrealism, to say nothing of free verse, were available to all; but I would venture to claim that what Blok did with symbolism, what Mayakovsky did with futurism, what Neruda did with surrealism, holds a lesson for us which we don't learn from our Yeats, Stevens, Pound or Eliot. The lesson . . . is related to the fact that literary movements should serve the ends of life as well as the ends of art." Mayakovsky's "With the Whole Voice" and Eliot's "Ash Wednesday" for instance both belong to 1930 and both mark important stages in their authors' development, but—"Mayakovsky's poem still crackles with a fierce life, while Eliot's has a dying charm. Why should the poem of the young suicide represent a victory, and the poem of the Nobel prize-winner and O.M. represent a defeat? The answer lies in the relation of a poet to the world he is living in." He draws a like distinction between Larkin's "Church Going" and Yevtushenko's "The Partisans' Graves," then castigates the local British failure. "This lack of serious care, this process of glossing over and softening, this lazy draping with a false timelessness, this distancing and dissolving of conflict—what are these but a fear of statement and commitment, a form of studied self-deprecation, a desperate disbelief in the power of poetry to speak out on man and society?" A further comparison, this time in the direction of the New World, offers a final flourish of defiance—"If you hear the record of Kerouac

16

reading his *October in the Railroad Earth* you know that the answer is Yes, whatever faults the writing has; if you read Tomlinson's *Seeing is Believing* you know that the answer must be No, whatever virtues the writing has."

Such an attitude could hardly be more different from the literary theories and practices of, say, the Movement or the Group, with their colonial expropriation of the definite article (like calling a magazine "*the* Review"). It must be remembered too that this was written before the so-called translation boom of the sixties, though just what effect that phenomenon has had on English poetry is difficult to say.[7] In the polemical context then the strokes are bold, the assertions one-sided, and there is no attempt to specify exactly how literary movements "should serve the ends of life as well as the ends of art," or how poetry can "speak out on man and society" in terms of who is saying what to whom and how he is saying it. Yet even allowing for the polemical context, this general attitude has been held consistently. The desire that poetry should "speak out" has been entertained seriously and responsibly, but it is not without a romantic element: it is not as passive as the notion of floating off to Timor, California or Saturn, but the fact is that those very questions which are raised but not answered in the Sovpoems preface are also raised, implicitly, in his own poetry, where they also remain, on those terms, unanswered.

A poem in which these questions are raised more explicitly than usual is "The Flowers of Scotland."[8] It first appeared in *Scottish International Review*, almost as a kind of editorial in verse, and the idea of such a purpose is quite in keeping with the possibilities that Morgan will entertain. But if the purpose of journalism is to "speak out" it does so on the basis of ascertained fact, the naming of names, and the poem tries to "speak out" by generalising to the point of caricature:

and bonny fechters kneedeep in dead ducks with all the
    thrawn intentness of the incorrigible professional Scot—

and the Scot here could be anyone, the Irishman in his bog, the Welshman in his valley, the Englishman in his castle. Where local particulars are mentioned they fail to make the argument any less general:

> and the unholy power of Grouse-moor and Broad-acres to
>   prevent the smoke of useful industry from sullying
>   Invergordon or setting up linear cities among the
>   whaups—
> and the banning of Beardsley and Joyce but not of course
>   of "Monster on the Campus" or "Curse of the Undead"—
>   those who think the former are the more degrading,
>   what are their values?—

Do we gain anything from substituting a useful-industry mentality for a grouse-moor mentality? And what about the language of this gesture: would any leader-writer commit that last sentence? And what do we make of:

> and dissidence crying in the wilderness to a moor of
>   boulders and two ospreys—

apart from referring to MacDiarmid's "Scotland Small?" which begins "Scotland small? Our multiform, our infinite Scotland *small?*" and after describing the variety to be observed under the apparent monotony of the moor landscape, ends " 'Nothing but heather!'—How marvellously descriptive. And incomplete!." [9] Assertion answers assertion and both are right, so who is speaking out to whom?

Nonetheless the stance represented is valuable, even if "The Flowers of Scotland" is an extreme instance. More recently he has described his literary orientation like this: "my own main interest as a poet is bound to centre on Scotland, and from there it will veer towards Voznesensky or Weöres or Creeley or Gomringer just as often as to any poet living in the south of England." And in another recent comment he has related this orientation to a view of Scotland compounded of negatives: "The difficulty is to write naturally. The Scottish air tends to be thick with advice and assertion, much of it hectoring, strident, unconsidered. Vehemence, and various sorts of fierceness, we have; but reason and thought and justice, and the stillness out of which a personality can grow to its full stretch without spikiness and shoulder-chips—these are harder to come by, and much to be desired . . . the step into freedom may be for the Scottish writer the hardest step. A residue of moral nervousness, a shying before images of joy or strangeness or abandon, can still cripple him with bonds that easily seem virtues. Obligations

18

bark at him on all sides as he goes down the path to the gate. There is so much that he is asked to, or may legitimately want to, relate himself to."[10] Again, the negatives may not be accurately related to specifically Scottish features (just *who* is hectoring and do we need to bother listening to him?) but they help to clarify a positive plea, for "the stillness out of which a personality can grow to its full stretch." This stillness is not necessarily to be achieved by speaking out (which can come close to hectoring), by being open to multifarious influences, or by welcoming the development of linear cities. It is difficult to come by anywhere. After all, the atmosphere of Timor will be thick, not just with advice, but with livid tropical poisons as well.

III

The autobiographical note which accompanied *Sovpoems*, written by a man of 40 and listing the romantic-sounding places he passed through mainly in his early twenties, is in keeping with the tone of the preface:

> Born Glasgow. Private in RAMC 1940–46. Storms round the Cape—oranges of Durban—tents and khamsin in Egyptian desert—hills of Sidon—Crusader castles—bug-ridden billets in Haifa—climbing Sannine—meditating in great Baalbeck. Visit to USSR 1955—rainy Leningrad to the blue Black Sea.

In his first published booklet of poems, *The Vision of Cathkin Braes* (Maclellan, Glasgow, 1952), the wide range is literary rather than geographical. The comic title poem, not always certain whether it is using or parodying its models, introduces Jenny Geddes, McGonagall, Knox, Lauren Bacall, Mary Queen of Scots, Mungo Park, Salome and Wordsworth, which motley crew pair off in the final episode like this: Lauren-Park, Jenny-Wordsworth, Salome-Knox, and Mary-McGonagall. There is a satirical sketch on modern dramatists, some Joycean word-play, a Gorky translation, and a couple of poems ("A Courtly Overture" and "A Snib for the Nones") which were recently reprinted, the latter being perhaps the most accomplished piece in the book.[11] While there is no recog-

19

nisably individual voice here, nor any cohesive group of interests, the strongest impressions are made by the verbal ingenuities and the varieties of style attempted.

The Cape of Good Hope, a long poem of 655 lines, then came in 1955 (Pound Press) in an edition of only 195 copies. It is an ambitious work, whose language (clearly that of a man who had recently translated *Beowulf*) and matter were quite at odds with the current run of English verse. The imagery owes a lot to the wartime voyaging mentioned in the above autobiographical note but what is striking about the poem is its sense of personal seriousness, a sense of urgency which compels the poet forward yet fails to reach a matching resolution. Looking back on the poem Morgan has said: "alienation was the keynote of the poem, solitude and the alienation of solitude, the difficulty of social adjustment. In that sense it's a very personal poem which I had to get out of my system. I think it probably doesn't work as well as I thought it was working at the time."[12] That is no doubt true, but the sense of unresolved personal seriousness, so strong here, is a quality frequently lacking in his more accomplished later verse. Since the work is virtually unknown, some description may be useful here.

In the opening lines of the first part, "The Cape"—

> Lands end, seas are unloosed, O my leviathan
> Libertinism, armoured sea-shoulderer, how you broke
> Out over foam and boulder! Break, ascetic man
> Like seas to cringing crag-hang home . . .

—we see at once where the clues "libertinism" and "ascetic" are pointing although their placing among the welter of realistic detail (as in the massive heaving third sentence which lifts us from line 4 to line 23) makes them look like helpless bobbing messages in bottles. When we come across a direct statement it may be simple and arresting—

> I chose the emptiness
> When fullness appalled me
>
> . . .
>
> The land rose withers
> As the land fruit rots
> But I barter autumn
> For what is seasonless

The second section, "Mid-Ocean," begins in strenuous excitement:

> When the grey cloud-haunches crouch, when the squall, the
>   night-loper
> Snarls to the sea, and the sea-blood shudders and curdles,
> And the growling and challenge burst from the throat of darkness,
> How glorious the beast's-coat of the constellations
> Wrinkling fierily to pounce, how splendid the fangs
> Bared with lightning that splinters the dense cross-drizzle
> And snaps above the shrinking troughs! . . .

and then gradually calms towards incantation. The heart of the
poem is the long third section, "A Dream at the Mysterious Barricades," the idea of barricades in the middle of the ocean being
rather an odd one but yet an accurate enough indication of what the
six characters in this part share: they have all, in a lonely or heroic
manner, reached an edge, a turning point, a revelation, a paradox.
Isolated they may be, but cumulatively they represent the heights
of human endeavour. First, Leonardo:

> What I love, I hate;
> What I make, unmake
> It is as much love
> When these arms embrace,
> As much creation
> When I plan bronzes
> Or princes' bridges
> As you will find love
> In the beating surf
> That is spent on sand
> Or generation
> In the slide and cling
> Of blue glacier
> And cold bridal hill.

Second, Michelangelo:

> In ogni loco God
> As prayed for came, and gazed
> Into desolation,
> Into a heart, into
> Michelangelo: once.

21

Third, Newton:

> Now the straw is on my back
> And dust rises from the track
> And the stellar day is black
> And knowledge is my burden
> . . .
> Walking in the universe
> I have lost the key of peace.

Beethoven, between symphonies six and seven is somewhat entangled in romantic cliches ("rapturous release," "irresistible joy," etc) but the loneliness is still there:

> And the love, the communion
> And the simplicity of love
> Unknown like the voices unheard
> Flooded his patience, and he wept.

Then Melville, plunging into his own symbolic oceans:

> But royal was Moby Dick, deeper
> Diving than symbol or sleight of thought;
> . . .
> He saw the singing throat choked with sea,
> The too stoic brow go down, the lips
> That praised their ships freeze by the ships wrecked.
> . . .
> —He rose, and lit the lamps; solitude
> Would return, solitude would return.

Finally, Mayakovsky:

> I see that those who praise life most are lost,
> Although their praise may keep whole worlds in faith;
> This sacrifice I understand at last.
> . . .
> Soviet, city, and friend, remember
> My voice and verse, and pardon in the hope
> The despair, for by the despair I spoke.

These experiences of isolation (in the midst of apparent fullness, it is worth stressing) indicate the real subject of the poem and it is debatable whether the apparatus of the voyage (in the midst of

emptiness) is necessary. Yet it is in the vigour, the sheer hard work and excitement in language, of this apparatus, in its description of departure from quotidian securities, that we sense the compulsion driving the poet. And in a similar way, although he avoids any explicit direct treatment of his own feelings of alienation, we sense the strength of these feelings in the magnitude of the figures he conjures up as analogies of his own condition. However, having launched into such deep waters it is difficult to see how he could resolve the poem in a manner true to those compulsions (Part IV— "The Return"). A temporary resolution for the poet through statement is one thing: a resolution which will hold in terms of the poem is quite another, despite the effort:

> Canvas, symphony, mural, poem, and law
> As searchlights swept from islands far off in life
> Stab and flush the echo-wakened memory
> And waken again its acknowledgement of solitude overcome
> In the work . . .

So it is understandable how the abstractions (materialism, love, hope, verity) come to be loaded with a weight which, in the poem, they cannot bear:

> This is the love that materiality
> Must learn, and this is the materiality
> That love must seize to be saved from despair.
> . . .
> For out of casting off he wins
> Arrival, and where he left his hope
> Trussed in the common human chains
> He journeys into the whole of verity . . .

It is possible that by this point in the poem these gestures were being made out of determination rather than compulsion.

IV

Morgan's next collection, and indeed his first substantial one, did not appear until 1968. *The Second Life* (Edinburgh University Press), about 70% of whose contents date from 1963–65, was one

23

of the most variegated collections to be published in the sixties. The design of the book itself only partly indicates this variety: there are three sections, for instance, on buff-coloured paper, of poems whose widely differing methods, purposes and levels of seriousness is not reflected by the tag "concrete." These sections separate four others, and although within each of these four there are no firm categories they do indicate four broad areas consistently explored by Morgan.

In general terms the themes in the first section are similar to those of *The Cape of Good Hope* but their treatment is now much less strenuous and their appeal to simple human values is a more credible and earned resolution than the earlier vague though desperate appeals to hope. The subjects of the first three poems, Hemingway, Marilyn Monroe and Edith Piaf, all attained a wide public following but this formal achievement in communication did not save them experiencing the extremes of isolation, extremes which in two cases led to suicide. Hemingway:

> No reassurance
> in that daybreak with no sun . . .

Monroe:

> Let no-one say communication is a cantword.
> They had to lift her hand from the bedside telephone.

Piaf:

> When you held me, your shoulders
> were a wall, I sheltered
> in your shadow, it began.

The first three poems are about human vulnerable figures. In "The Domes of Saint Sophia" we have invulnerable perfected form which through achieving such perfection has lost human relevance. The idea in:

> What time has barely kept
> let that be the most dearly kept

is one which recurs in "London," a poem to be discussed later. Here, the domes

24

                          give no grip
                    to the searching mind
                    in its trouble.
                    I take no assurance
                    from a soaring vault.

Then, in "The White Rhinoceros" and "The Third Day of the Wolf"
we have the non-human animals, but they too are vulnerable,
almost hopelessly so, in the face of the human predators. After
such permutations of human, inhuman, vulnerable, invulnerable,
there is a further plea for the value of the human scale, like the
earlier one in favour of ruins (that speak) rather than domes (which
remain silent). This scale may be measured against cosmic geological
dimensions—

    A dead child or a busker or a bobbin-winder
    cries through the raised beaches and the disinterested
    eternity of the foraminifera.   ("To Hugh MacDiarmid")

Or it may be measured in terms of craftsmanship, though a very
different kind of craftsmanship from that which produced the domes
of St Sophia—

                    You give the pleasure
                    of made things,
                    the construction holds
                    like a net, or it
                    unfolds in waves
                    a certain measure,
                    of affection.   ("To Ian Hamilton Finlay")

A recurring image worth mentioning is that of the mist, generally
denoting the obscurity of a hostile environment. In "The Old
Man and the Sea" the first sentence rolls through 19 lines like the
mist it describes rolling in from the Pacific. Piaf waits in a circle of
rain. The wolf flees its pursuers in the mist. In "To Ian Hamilton
Finlay"

                    Scotland is
                    the little bonfires
                    in cold mist . . .

In "Aberdeen Train," by contrast, the mist helps to frame a little
picture, of a pheasant looking at a glinting piece of glass—"a

25

Chinese moment in the Mearns"—but in the following miniature, "The Opening of the Forth Road Bridge," the mist again signifies original chaos, through which man the constructor must make his way.

The concerns in this first group are thus clearly stated, both locally and in the ordering of the poems. The desire to "speak out," or at least to be readily accessible, is evident in other ways. The nearer he is to home ground (Hugh MacDiarmid, Ian Hamilton Finlay, Maurice Lindsay) the more individual his characters become; but the further away (Hemingway, Monroe, Piaf) the more he relies on cliches from the popular image, and this reliance seems to be deliberate. The use of verbal cliches seems to be equally deliberate —"the shot / insulted the morning," "a great writer's life," "the inhuman valleys" (Hemingway); "broad shoulders," "firm mouth" of the man Piaf is waiting for; "soaring vault," "foundered columns" (St Sophia); "flashing past gardens," "padding along a highway" (the wolf). The surfaces of these poems (as of many others) is designed to offer least resistance to the reader or listener. Again, the frequent resort to imperatives implies some awareness of, or attitude towards, an audience, as in "The Domes of Saint Sophia" (*waken*), "The White Rhinoceros" (*save, watch, smash*), "The Third Day of the Wolf (*take care, beware*), "The Opening of the Forth Road Bridge" (*fold, break, make*). The extreme example of audience-awareness is "The Death of Marilyn Monroe," whose repeated exclamations sound as if they are echoing in a very large but very empty hall.

V

This desire for ease of communication is also evident in the second grouping, the Glasgow poems, with their jostling street-scenes of gaiety ("Linoleum Chocolate," "Trio"), fear ("The Suspect") and pathos ("Good Friday," "In the Snack-Bar"). Again, their ordering allows for a cumulative effect. And again, their leitmotiv is sounded at the outset ("To Joan Eardley"):

Such rags and streaks
that master us!

History and its bitter residue is inevitable ("King Billy") yet while

the memories of partisan violence and the ambivalent nostalgias
are recognised as contemporary facts this poem moves from description to injunction, ending:

> Go from the grave. The shrill flutes
> are silent, the march dispersed.
> Deplore what is to be deplored,
> and then find out the rest.

Once more the imperatives imply both an audience and a certain
didactic purpose ("speaking out") in that it concludes with a plea
for a general change of attitude. This tension between the recognition
of fact and the plea for renewal is heightened in "Glasgow Green"
as it moves through modulated description to incantation. The
latter reaches its climax in

> Water the wilderness, walk there, reclaim it!
> Reclaim, regain, renew! Fill the barns and the vats!

If the poem had ended there we would have been left rather high
in the air, wondering just what, in precise social terms, such an
injunction could mean. But the conclusion, without contradicting
the validity of the wish, recognises things as they are:

> Longing,
>> longing
>>> shall find its wine.
> Let the women sit in the Green
> and rock their prams as the sheets
> blow and whip in the sunlight.
> But the beds of married love
> are islands in a sea of desire.
> Its waves break here, in this park,
> splashing the flesh as it trembles
> like driftwood through the dark.

"In the Snack-Bar" then describes a confrontation with a human
ruin who is the victim of nature rather than of human violence:
a blind hunchback in a cafe, who has to be helped to the toilet.
The relentless fact-by-fact account of the incident holds back
embarrassment, pity and disgust until towards the end a simile
focusses a reaction blended of distaste and fascination:

Does he know how frightening he is in his strangeness
under his mountainous coat, his hands like wet leaves
stuck to the half-white stick?

Ruins may speak, in contrast to the silent domes (of St Sophia):
but here it is the clamped impossibility of communication with the
human ruin which forces an exclamation from the poet—"Dear
Christ, to be born for this!"

The more recent "Glasgow Sonnets"[13] explore similar territory.
The exigencies of form can be a hindrance—

> The man lies late since he has lost his job,
> smokes on one elbow, letting his coughs fall
> thinly into an air too poor to rob.

—but they can also allow for gradations of pace and tone such as this:

> A shilpit dog fucks grimly by the close.
> Late shadows lengthen slowly, slogans fade.

The generally hard-edged manner still accommodates personifications such as "a mean wind wanders," "hackles on puddles rise,"
"the kettle whimpers," "the great sick Clyde shivers in its bed."
It is noticeable that such imagery relates to the old down-trodden
side of the city, whereas the "developments" evoke a sharper
description—

> Vistas swim out from the bulldozer's bite
> by day, and banks of earthbound stars at night
> begin . . .
> . . .
> A multi is a sonnet stretched to ode
> and some say that's no joke . . .

But the focus is primarily on the stalled lives:

> They linger in the single-ends that use
> their spirit to the bone, and when they trudge
> from closemouth to laundrette their steady shoes
> carry a world that weighs us like a judge.

And here is the ambivalence characteristic of any attempt to write
poetry directly about the human aspects of a giant social problem—

the unresolved tension between a sense of responsibility (the subject-matter is real and urgent) and a sense of irrelevance (is a slum-dweller or an unemployed family-man likely to be remotely interested in *poetry* about his plight?).

> Hugh MacDiarmid forgot
> in "Glasgow 1960" that the feast
> of reason and the flow of soul had ceased
> to matter to the long unfinished plot
> of heating frozen hands. We never got
> an abstruse song that charmed the raging beast.

No doubt, but in MacDiarmid's case this (equally unresolved) contradiction was part of his dialectical zigzagging; it was grist to his mill. In Morgan's case, many of the Glasgow poems raise the question of how the security of a highly-literate, multi-lingual university lecturer *belongs* to an environment of "stalled lives?" In a metropolis there are hundreds of different ways of belonging. They overlap, but they may still be universes apart.

A very different Glasgow poem, "Rider,"[14] will reinforce the point. Here we have a grotesque apocalyptic mêlée—

> a giant hedgehog lifting the Necropolis/solid silver/to the moon/
>   sang of the deluge
> long keys of gas unlocked the shaking Campsies at/last, at least/
>   four drumlins were heard howling/as far as Fenwick Moor . . .

We have literary jokes—

> Davidson looked through the telescope at MacDiarmid and said/
>   what, is that God

referring to MacDiarmid's poem "Of John Davidson" which ends:

> —A bullet-hole through a great scene's beauty,
> God through the wrong end of a telescope.[15]

The cast includes Lucretius (en route from the Crab Nebula), Orpheus, and various lesser lights of strictly local fame, and these disparate elements tend to pull the poem apart at its edges like the ragged perimeter of a whirlpool. The force operates most effectively when it is within restricted bounds:

29

butcher-boys tried to ward off sharks/the waters rose quickly/
    great drowned bankers
floated from bay-windows/two housemaids struggled on
    Grosvenor Terrace with a giant conger
the Broomielaw was awash with slime and torn-out claws and
    anchor-flakes/rust and dust
sifted together where a dredger ploughed up the Gallowgate/
    pushed a dirty wave over Shettleston
spinning shopfronts crashed in silence/grassily, massively/
    porticoes tilting/settled in mud
lampreys fastened on four dead sailors drifting through Finnieston
    /in a Drygate attic . . .

Morgan belongs to *this* Glasgow as much as to any other, and perhaps he is more at home here, for all that King Billy would recognise
next to nothing.

VI

The second and third groups may be considered together, for
they both develop themes implicit in the title of the book: renewal
(second life) both cosmic, as man reaches into space, urban, as the
slums are cleared, and personal, as an individual man experiences
and records the simplicities of a close relationship. The title poem
celebrates seasonal renewal as well:

> green May, and the slow great blocks rising
> under yellow tower cranes, concrete and glass and steel
> out of a dour rubble it was and barefoot children gone—
> Is it only the slow stirring, a city's renewed life
> that stirs me, could it stir me so deeply
> as May, but could May have stirred
> what I feel of desire and strength
> like an arm saluting a sun?

But the implied answer is no, for the "second eye" which is remaking
what it sees derives its strength from a deeper source. The vision
of urban renewal also suggests a wide context, and the poem ends
with a characteristically general injunction:

30

A great place and its people are not renewed lightly.
The caked layers of grime
grow warm, like homely coats.
But yet they will be dislodged
and men will still be warm.
The old coats are discarded.
The old ice is loosed.
The old seeds are awake.

Slip out of darkness, it is time.

"The Unspoken" then narrows down the field of vision toward
particular experience. First, there is the memory of a moment of
exaltation, but in contradictory circumstances—

and the dawn came up like thunder like that moon drawing the
water of our yearning
though we were going to war, and left us exalted,
that was happiness,
but it is not like that.

With an eye to the future, and with "cheeks burning with old
Promethean warmth," again with the closeness of new-life and old-
death, there is
an animal
strapped in a doomed capsule, but the future
was still there, cool and whole like the moon,
waiting to be taken, smiling even
as the dog's bones and the elaborate casket of aluminium
glow white and fuse in the arc of re-entry,
and I knew what I felt was history . . .

But in neither instance is "it" (the unspoken) "like that." What
"it" *is* like, experienced "without a name," can be approached
only in terms of personal contact, though here again there is a
similar kind of osmosis between fear and joy:

when I stole a glance at your face as we stood in a doorway and
found I was afraid
of what might happen if I should never see it again . . .
. . .

31

> . . . and as you shifted in my arms
> it was the sea changing the shingle that changes it
> as if for ever . . .

The short love-poems which now follow ("From a City Balcony,"
"When You Go," "Strawberries," "One Cigarette," "The Picnic,"
"Absence") gain an added dimension from the context thus prepared. Individually they recount the most simple incidents, in
language which aims not to complicate the simplicity. As we have
seen already, the directness of Morgan's language may entail the
use of cliches and in this group we find examples like "pale stars
winking," "crisp cold evenings" ("The Second Life"), "a deep
confusion of feelings," "stole a glance" ("The Unspoken"), "the
day grows bright," "a sparkling burn," "blaze of gorse" ("From
a City Balcony"), "sultry afternoon," "hot sunlight" ("Strawberries"), "wind swirling the curtains" ("Absence"). There is the
occasional falter into a rather grotesque "poetic" cliche ("looming
mastery/that lays its hand on the young man's bowels"), and the
temptations of ad-language are not invariably resisted ("the drowsy
country thing").
    The penultimate poem in the section confirms the context of
small fallible human realities giving us a home in monstrous wastes:
for all its promise and excitement, the prospect of space *is* monstrous
and among the "electronic yelling from Andromeda" and the
"spikes/of anti-matter"

> you'd give a world
> for a stream of human lies,
> because they could be lies.

Despite the "grave of dreams," the "desolation without dimension,"

> . . . everything is in its place, the pinch of clover
> from a summer field could break the heart.
> Subsist in iron, and wait.

The three science-fiction poems in the last section explore a very
similar pattern—of enormous distances and possibilities in time and
space acquiring any possible human relevance only in relation to
the age-old human strengths and weaknesses we bring with us.
The distances are certainly alluring and seem to demand the romantic
gesture—

32

Take the voyage out then! Drink the milk of space!
Let the night break like a shell—throw it behind you.
And let the great islands of space, which are not clouds
Magellanic or earthly, be your morning landfall.

The call of Timor again—and if we reached Timor, what then?
Electronic yelling? Old war-wounds? "In Sobieski's Shield," a
poem of 99 long lines, imagines the rematerialisation of a family
in a remote part of the universe (the SF mechanics are of secondary
interest) and asks what survives. The tentativeness of the awakening
is enacted in the movement of the loose-limbed yet hesitant verse,
which could have been punctuated into regular sentences but instead
is broken into lines whose length hovers between 11 and 15 syllables.
The awakening is into a kind of second life. The father is narrator:

> . . . second life I don't
> know what made me use that phrase who are we
> if we are not who we were we have only
> one life . . .

Of the son:

> . . . his blue eyes
> are the same but there's a new graveness of the
> second life that phrase again . . .

The rematerialisation is not perfect (a missing finger, a missing nipple)
yet it seems also to have transferred features not previously possessed:

> . . . and one most curious
> I almost said birthmark and so it is in a sense
> light brown shaped like a crazy heart spreading
> across my right forearm well let it be . . .

And this "birthmark" has in fact been rematerialised from a tattoo
on a dead arm held up out of the mud of Flanders in the Great War:

> . . . I have
> a graft of war and ancient agony forgive
> me my dead helper

They have unwittingly carried their history with them and that
too is part of the harsh new environment they must explore—

33

"it's hard/to go let's go," ends the poem, the injunction this time held within the poem and not directed outwards at an audience.

"From the Domain of Arnheim" complements this forward journey with one back in time. What the explorers interrupt is not a terrifying primordial rite but simple joy over a birth.

> To them we were a displacement of the air,
> a sudden chill, yet we had no power
> over their fear. If one of them had been dying
> he would have died . . .

A sweating trumpeter throws a brand at where their bodies would have been and they feel "nothing but his courage." So they return with more than scientific tokens (rocks, seeds): they bring back human tokens, "deeper souvenirs."

VII

Morgan's so-called concrete poems[16] have often been a sticking-point for reviewers who dislike having their categories questioned or who cannot accept that play may be serious. The borderline between these and his "ordinary" poems is very fluid[17] and the apparent differences in method belie a close continuity of thematic exploration. Their sheer variety eludes purist classifications and they are most naturally seen as extensions in several directions of processes in his "ordinary" poetry. A piece like "Starryveldt," a word list running through "Sharpeville," "spoorvengeance," "scattervoortrekker," etc to "so:VAEVICTIS," is "about real experience" just as much as the Glasgow poems are, and whether it is syntactical or not is a secondary matter. "Archives," with its column of the words "generation upon" eaten away from the bottom as by moth and age, like an ancient banner hanging in a cathedral, could make its point no other way.[18] In some of the jokes, visual effect is all, as in "Surfeit" where the word "lamprey" coils around in intestinal lumps; in others, sound is all, as in "The Loch Ness Monster's Song" or "Eohippus."[19] In the "emergent poems" the very process of reading is an integral part of the effect: in these, the single complete line towards which the poem emerges is printed at the bottom of the page and from the letters used other

34

words are derived, but the letters stay in their column positions thus giving an apparently scattered effect. It is a sophisticated version of the game "see how many words you can make from the letters of *zeugma*," and the ingenuity involved is considerable. If we take "Seven Headlines" and unscatter the superstructure we get:

1. old solemn ode sold for fender iron
2. bold trend in letter to solo reader
3. arson from bolt from blue
4. absent food bud found
5. utter ferment in reason
6. team feed at modern lode
7. no fetter for absolute modern men

And the base line from which these have been derived and towards which they emerge is "il faut être absolument moderne." In "Message Clear" we have a more serious undertaking as we chart the obscure and hesitant progress of the lower-case "i" towards the clarity of "i am the resurrection and the life." The scrambling effect is only apparent since each letter must stay in its column and the labour of the eye as it reads is an enactment of what the poem is about. If we unscramble again, this is what we find:

/am i/if/i am he/hero/hurt/there and/here and/here/and/there/
i am rife/in/sion and/i die/am ere sect/am ere section/of/the
life/of/men/sure/the die/is/set and/i am the surd/at rest/
o life/i am here/i act/i run/i meet/i tie/i stand/i am thoth/
i am ra/i am the sun/i am the son/i am the erect one if/i am rent/
i am safe/i am sent/i heed/i test/i read/a thread/a stone/a
tread/a throne/i resurrect/a life/i am in life/i am resurrection/
i am the resurrection and/i am/i am the resurrection and the life[20]

"Manifestations of the questing spirit" is how Morgan has referred to such forays into the possibilities of concrete, sound and found poetry.[21] The found elements play an important part, even if they are only the oddities of word-construction, and an interesting extension of such "manifestations" can be seen in the more recent "instamatic poems," where the found elements are actual events. Morgan describes these poems as being "based upon actual things which have happened as reported in the news-

35

papers or on television. I try to imagine somebody had been there with an instamatic camera, and quickly taken a photograph. The whole thing is presented directly in economic, visual terms. I try not to add comment, but there's a very careful presentation which very often does include a kind of invisible comment."[22] The recording of date and place testify to the documentary truth— i.e. the subject of the poem is from "real life" as recorded by on-the-spot reporters and what better material could a poet who wants to "speak out" have? Since the supply of incidents is endless it may appear that the possible production of instamatic poems is also endless, but the poet here is not quite the camera he says he is. The comment is not really invisible: the absence of direct comment *is* very noticeable, especially when the calmly narrated story is gruesome, as in the case of the man killing himself with a power-drill or in the case of the villagers preparing to eat a python which has already eaten a boy.[23] But even where there is no frisson between the sensational story and the matter-of-fact voice, the selection and ordering of detail, the tone and the rhythm all serve to control our responses as deliberately as ever. Indeed, what we are most conscious of is the feeling of being controlled: "just look at this!" What we do not feel is a sense of the poet exploring his own responses: these are implicit only in the directions in which he draws our attention, so while the focus may be sharp, the camera can swing only within a narrow arc.

VIII

The habitual concerns that bind Morgan's poetry are clear enough. The lure of Timor, in many guises, is welcomed: but ambiguously, for the stronger commitment is to "what time has barely kept," to the "rags and streaks," to the human possibilities of the life here and now "care of the black roofs." The kind of vision which he attributes to MacDiarmid, wherein the enormities of space and time are somehow never big enough to dwarf basic human simplicities, is his too:

> A dead child or a busker or a bobbin-winder
> cries through the raised beaches and the disinterested
> eternity of the foraminifera . . .

or through the "electronic yelling from Andromeda."

What is less clear is the relation of his own personality to its protean but partial manifestations. He may not assume masks such as dramatic personae but his many different modes of expression seem to serve a like function: are they ways of *saying* or ways of *hiding*? Technically, at the level of performance, he seems capable of tackling anything and bringing it off. Much of his work has the coolness of virtuosity, for although his concerns are seriously and coherently explored, he remains, unlike Iain Crichton Smith for instance, an unobsessive poet. Crichton Smith's poetry lives at the nerve-ends of an exposed personality reacting to raw experience; when he fails it is as if he suddenly jitters sideways into the darkness and we lose sight of him. When Morgan fails it is as if his efficient intelligence were planning a space-shot and calculating the chances down to the minimum.

The possibilities remain wide open, but the more interesting of them will show not so much yet further diversification but perhaps a drawing together. And here, finally, it is worth referring to "London,"[24] a dense, highly-wrought poem in three parts which succeeds in accommodating many of his habitual concerns and whose linguistic variety is an integral part of that accommodation. An indication of its scope can be gathered if we follow, briefly, just one of the poem's many threads. Part I ("St James' Park") begins in relaxation:

> Who could sleep in London's orient wheat,
> yet I think we fell asleep.

Time imprisons and ages us, but if the prison walls were to dissolve would we really be free? Would we not then be even more helplessly imprisoned in a kaleidoscope of dreams? It turns: desires, fears, and seasons tumble. The dreams entice:

> Going there was
> pure—like into blue very highland air.

They also menace; with hints of the second life again:

> through tall windows
> trees hung like spectres of the next life.

>   . . .

> You are not afraid
> of a few icy trees, but we are both afraid
> of what is happening to us.

Dream-figures offer satisfactions (water, linen, oranges) to assuage the droughts of nightmare, but they are rejected.

Part 2 ("Soho"—subtitled "Humanae Vitae") turns a different kaleidoscope: throughout 52 lines, scraps of advertisements are combined and permutated, now and then clarifying into jokes like "original sex carpet," "ABZ of unrepeatable tropic of enemas," "an unhurried view of impotence rock plants and alpines," etc. Those phrases that do cohere into a recognisable meaning appear to be just as "found" as those that do not and the sheer quantity of the material in this section, keeping the subtitle in mind, is reminiscent of the multitudinousness of humanity that we find in medieval allegories. The conglomeration, which could continue indefinitely, comes to rest in a line that allows all this material to be drawn into the context of the whole poem:

> slightly washable shop soiled down the ages

> But to wash London
> would take a sea.
> To want to wash it
> history.

> Now bury this poem in one of the vaults
> of our civilisation . . .

In the first section we have the involuntary private dreams of the park: ways of floating off to Timor. In the second we have the public bartered dreams of the market-place: not floating this time but buying and selling grubby tickets. Then in Part 3 we look down over the intricate metropolitan panorama from the Post Office Tower, from a pinnacle of urban technological development, from a listening post which gives us access to messages from space (perhaps we can bounce messages off Timor?). But this is no god's eye view. As we listen to the messages that

> break in rings
> of strange accident
> and mortal change

38

we realise how the human dreams and worries, the fatal work of the seasons, cannot be escaped; we just see them more clearly. On a roof an old man sits on a chair watching linen flowers on a washing-line; the flowers are "tugging to be free." Nearby, poised "like some fine insect," a young man adjusts the arms of a TV aerial "into the path of their messages."

>—And all that grace to dwindle to
> a faded dressing-gown, a kitchen chair in the sun.

These new roofs with their gardens, vistas and aerials are not like the old black ones, but the humans who exist "care of" them are unmistakably recognisable.

Notes

S.L.—*The Second Life* (Edinburgh University Press, 1968).

G.S.—*From Glasgow to Saturn* (Carcanet Press, 1973).

P.—Penguin Modern Poets No. 15 (1969).

L.R.—*Lines Review.*

N.E.R.—*New Edinburgh Review* No. 19 (August 1972).

S.I.R.—*Scottish International Review.*

1. *N.E.R.*, p. 14.

2. *G.S.*, p. 10.

3. Many of his translations are scattered in a wide variety of magazines and a collection is overdue. Translations in book-form include: *Beowulf* (Hand and Flower Press 1952, University of California Press 1962); *Poems from Eugenio Montale* (University of Reading School of Art 1959); *Sovpoems* (Migrant Press 1961); *Sándor Weöres: Selected Poems* (Penguin Books 1970); *Wi the haill voice: 25 poems by Mayakovsky* (Carcanet Press 1972).

4. I have illustrated some of the details in my review of *Wi the haill voice* in *S.I.R.*, August 1972.

5. See his article "Heraclitus in Gorky Street," *S.I.R.*, January 1968, and my review of Reavey's *The New Russian Poets* in *S.I.R.*, January 1969. There do seem to be possibilities in Scots for Voznesensky—see R. Watson's versions in *L.R.* 36, Spring 1971.

6. See G. Gömöri, *Polish and Hungarian Poetry 1945–1956* (OUP, 1966), *passim*. Also the interview with Weöres in *Tri-Quarterly* No. 9 (Spring 1967).

7. Is it symptomatic for instance that there is virtually no discussion in *British Poetry since 1960* (Carcanet Press, 1972) of foreign poetry, either as a matter of interest in itself or as an obvious and fruitful source of cross-fertilisation? Both Jon Silkin and Peter Porter touch on this, the former with both sympathy and considerable editorial experience, yet both of them seem to be overawed by the *dangers* of translation. For most of the other contributors these dangers are avoided simply by avoiding foreigners.

8. *P.*, pp. 145–46.

9. Hugh MacDiarmid, *Collected Poems* (Macmillan, 1967), pp. 423–24.

10. *The Review*, tenth anniversary issue, 1972, p. 54; and *British Poetry since 1960*, p. 132. See also "The Resources of Scotland," *T.L.S.*, 28.7.72, pp. 885–86.

11. *P.*, pp. 156, 157.

12. *N.E.R.*, p. 12.

13. *G.S.*, pp. 92 ff; they have also been published as a booklet by Castlelaw Press, West Linton, Peeblesshire.

14. *S.I.R.*, November 1972.

15. *Collected Poems*, p. 284.

16. There are 20 examples in *S.L.*, and more can be found in *Emergent Poems* (Hansjorg Mayer, 1967), *Gnomes* (Akros, 1968) and *The Horseman's Word* (Akros, 1970).

17. See for instance the varieties of "song" in *Twelve Songs* (Castlelaw, 1970), which have also been collected in *G.S.*

18. *S.L.*, p. 23 and *Gnomes*, p. 3.

19. *Gnomes*, p. 4; *G.S.*, p. 35; *The Horseman's Word*, p. 7.

20. *S.L.*, pp. 49, 24–25.

21. *The Review*, as above.

22. *N.E.R.*, p. 14.

23. *L.R. 42/43*, pp. 16, 20; and *Instamatic Poems* (Ian McKelvie, 1973), pp. 19, 21.

24. *G.S.*, p. 37.

II

IAIN CRICHTON SMITH

THE MOST CHARACTERISTIC effects of Iain Crichton Smith's poetry
depend on his individual and at times idiosyncratic manner of
juxtaposing images. This manner is best described in two phrases
of his own, though both were used of other people's poems. The
first was an approving comment on one of Maurice Lindsay's verses:

the logic is true but not foreseen[1]

and the second was a description of the effect of MacDiarmid's
lyric "The Watergaw:"

a kind of shock is achieved which goes beyond logic.[2]

In each case what attracted him in the other man's work was an
effect he constantly aims at in his own. In *The Golden Lyric* this
personal attraction is all the more evident for his lack of sympathy
with the whole trend of MacDiarmid's later work: his critical
assumptions in that direction are inhibiting, but his comment on the
unexpected combination of images in "The Watergaw" (rainbow
and dying face) is clearly applicable to very similar effects throughout
his own poetry. The first element of this effect is surprise, at the
apparent affront to our logical expectations, and the second element
is a kind of revelation, a discovery of vibrant possibilities with a
logic of their own.

Two short poems will exemplify. In the first, No. 31 of a
sequence called "Transparencies," the poet's wry and jocose self-
regard is suddenly undercut by a much chillier kind of self-regard.

I would love
to write
a "great" poem,
big as the Cuillins.
Instead,
I sniff a yellow rose,
a great yellow
bourgeois
garden rose.

And I stick a
carnation in my
buttonhole.
Deep red inside,
pink outside.

> I thrust my cuffs out.
> They are like the blur
> of autumn
> at the edge of a
> leaf.[3]

The simile yokes together two apparently incongruous images: the cuff (artificial, a sign of human ostentation) and the autumn leaf (natural, a sign of inevitable decay). When our attention has been arrested by this incongruity the separate connotations of each image then overlap—the tension generated is like that built up by an electric current before a spark leaps across a gap.

The second poem is called "Old Woman with Flowers"—

> These are your flowers. They were given to you
> so nurse them carefully and tenderly.
> Though flowers grow freely elsewhere, here in this room
> there's not much space, so therefore like a child
> let no-one else go near them.
>   O dear God
> wherever you are, I am almost driven wild
> by your frightening flowers whose blossoms are turned to bone
> for an old woman to look at, in a small room alone.[4]

The *raison d'être* of this short poem is the juxtaposition of "blossom" and "bone:" again, the incongruity startles, but in the context prepared by the first part of the poem, what then continues to startle us is not the mere incongruity but the agonised perception inherent in this moment. A similar image, in similar circumstances, recurs in the novel *The Last Summer*, when the protagonist Malcolm visits a friend who is dying of T.B.—

> "Have you got the draughtboard?" said Malcolm, in the same cheerful voice which seemed to ring hollowly through the house, echoing among the dead white ornaments, which included a bouquet of marblish flowers and a gipsy's cart full of needles.[5]

Granted, there is no overt clash of disparate images here, for the flowers referred to are not real anyway: but the impact of *dead*, *white* and *marblish* as applied, in this context, even to imitation flowers, implies that Malcolm in his imagination is already painfully aware of what is happening to his friend.

Despite their small scale, the two poems quoted illustrate the way in which Crichton Smith prepares for the placing of such imagery. This can best be described in terms of two kinds of language. The first is colloquial, explanatory, discursive; it describes situations, ruminates, asks questions, generalises; it is the normal functional language of his poetry, a language which allows the verse to follow the sometimes devious movements of his mind. The second is much more condensed and resonant, though it seldom disrupts our syntactical expectations: what surprises us is the ellipsis in the thought, the unexpected associations, often heightened indeed by the very orderliness of the syntax. The timing and placing of the movement from the first kind of language to the second is of crucial importance to the over-all effect of individual poems. In the two examples quoted, this movement is simple: in each case it occurs towards the end of the poem, after the context has been prepared. When the timing of such a movement is judged with less certainty the result is either a preponderance of the first kind of language (resulting in loss of tension) or a preponderance of the second (resulting in opacity a too cryptic presentation).

The short poem "Pain" will illustrate my point:

> Thorny fish from the rotting rocks.
> The fish sabre each other.
>
> I look down from clear pain
> on to the slime's arena.
>
> I have left the world behind
> I am become a new moon.[6]

Now in its original form, among the material from which *Lines Review* No. 29 was compiled, this poem was called "Toothache" and consisted of 24 lines. As a whole this original poem sagged because it offered too much explanation of an unremarkable kind, and those three separate couplets were misplaced and mistimed: yet I suggested that these images were worth saving. The poem as it stands, while by no means opaque, still has a kind of density not characteristic of Crichton Smith: he would normally give us more of an explicit context.

* * *

45

An earlier poem, "Sunday Morning Walk," and a passage from the novel *Consider the Lilies* will illustrate a further aspect of Crichton Smith's handling of his imagery: the obsessive attention directed towards certain images, a fascination that persists whether or not thematic abstractions are from time to time made.

In "Sunday Morning Walk"[7] the poet leaves behind "the tall black men and their women walking/over the tight-locked streets" and strolls into the open countryside; his imagination ponders on the coupling of Jove and Leda.

And occupied thus, I came where a dead sheep lay
close to a fence, days gone. The flies were hissing and buzzing
out of the boiling eyes, wide open as day.
I stood in the sunlight beside it, watching and musing.

Three crows famished yards off. Live sheep grazed far
from the rotting carcass. The jaw, well-shaved, lay slackly
there on the warm quiet grass. The household air
was busy with buzzing like fever. How quickly, how quickly

the wool was peeled from the back! How still was the flesh!
How the visiting flies would not knock at the door of the sockets!
How the hole in the side gaped red, a well-sized gash!
How the clear young lambs grazed in the shade of the thickets!

And the sun blazed hot on my shoulder. Here was no shade.
But the sheep was quiet, so quiet. There was nothing to notice
but the grape-bunched flies and the crows. Could a world have
    stayed
if I'd taken a stick in my hand to beat off the flies?

A certain slackness is not unusual in the earlier work, yet, while these lines could easily be tautened, their repetitiveness helps to confirm our impression of a desire to linger on this image, to look and look and savour every aspect of its appearance ("the household air," "grape-bunched flies," etc). The presence in the poem of the Sunday town, of the day-dreams about Jove and Leda, and of the dead sheep itself, can be accounted for in terms of the structure of the poem and of the relations implied between these three groups of images—what cannot be accounted for so readily is the fascinated stare in these lines, as if much more is sensed than can be brought within the compass of this particular poem. The slightly nervous and defensive gesture in the last line quoted is like a deliberate attempt to break the spell. The poem ends:

The flies in the wound continued their occupied sound
as I turned my back on a death of no weeping or mourning.

But he does return to the same image, most notably in the central chapter of *Consider the Lilies*, the chapter which describes the turning point in Mrs Scott's life: her encounter with the minister and the effect upon her of his refusal to see the evictions from her point of view. To reach the manse she has to walk across the moor and halfway through the description of this journey the focus alters:

Seen from above she was a diminutive figure in black plodding steadily across the moor alive with yellow and wine-red . . .

Then:

. . . she came suddenly upon an object which at first she took to be a piece of dirty cloth. As she approached it she could hear a thick buzzing sound which puzzled her, a buzzing as of a great number of flies, almost like the sound of a sleepy saw sawing fresh wood. When she came to the object she looked down and almost turned away with disgust and sickness. It was the carcass of a thin sheep, soiled white with a black head, one of the Highland sheep of which people owned one or two. But nevertheless she stayed there for a while, fascinated with feelings of revulsion and pity. The sheep stared up at her, both its sockets empty and yet liquid as if with tears. The crows could have done that and indeed as she looked she saw a crow some yards off, staring at her stonily with fixed eyes as if there was real intelligence behind them. There was a gash in the sheep's side at which the flies were buzzing in a domestic sort of way. In fact it all looked very homely. The buzzing reminded her of the humming of Sunday pots on boil. All the living beings she could see—which were the flies—were busy, all except the sheep whose black legs were twisted under it and the crow which was waiting for her to go, as if it had staked a claim to the place. Now that she could see it more clearly she noticed that its thin black head was twisted on its neck at an unnatural angle. It was quite quite dead and yet in a disturbing way it seemed to be appealing to her out of its empty sockets. The flies of course didn't notice she was there. They hummed fatly and richly at the wound. [8]

Some verbal parallels with "A Sunday Morning Walk" will be noticed at once ("the household air"—"domestic" and "homely") and the fascination clearly felt by the narrator in the poem is openly attributed to Mrs Scott in the novel. Yet why is this image here, at this point in the story? It is difficult to see any fictional necessity for its use. I doubt very much if the sheep is meant in any way to "symbolise" the fate of the highlanders, for such a crude analogy would be alien to Crichton Smith's habits. Granted, there is an effective reference back to the incident, when Mrs Scott is beginning to realise the implications of the minister's "betrayal"—

> ... And perhaps because of the eyes, which remained cold though they appeared to twinkle, or a trick of the light, or the way his head was cocked, or was it perhaps because of the buzzing of a fly on the window-pane, she was reminded of the crow which had stared unwinkingly at her, only rising at the last moment, as she had left the dead and dreadfully wounded sheep behind. The buzzing of the flies seemed still to be at her ears. [9]

But the incident can hardly be accounted for as a pretext for a back-reference. For again we have the *fascination*, the *stare*, the lingering sense of an image (an image of a brute fact) whose significance cannot be unravelled. It obtrudes into the narrative because it obtrudes into the poet's imagination.

* * *

Crichton Smith's manner of juxtaposing apparently dissimilar images, and the obsessive nature of his attention to certain images, largely determine the characteristic movement of his poems. This movement is carried forward not so much by "linear" progression (development of a theme, variations on a theme) as by a series of diversions, a zigzag pattern. More careful writers may be more punctilious about "keeping to the point," about refusing to be led off at unexpected tangents. But as Crichton Smith himself has said:

> I don't like poets who are in complete control of their poems, because it seems to me that they're making objects. I like the

poetry where the people are not in full control, because if you are in full control of a poem as a conscious object, then it's finished.[10]

And in a different context he has put the point this way:

Actually, the kind of poetry that I would have liked to write would have been the kind of poetry where there would be metrical ideas of harmony and music, which at the same time would be under siege by a kind of barbaric emotional power, which would almost destroy the metrical harmony, but would not be able to accomplish it.[11]

This is not a question of relaxation, or submitting to distractions for their own sake, but rather a question of how far the poet can (to use one of MacDiarmid's definitions) let the movement of his verse express the movement of his mind. It is also a question of how far the poet is willing, in his poetry, to be exposed to the raw experiences of his life, and this is a point to which I shall return.

In the meantime, the poem "On a Summer's Day" will illustrate this progress through diversion, this ability to follow the most disparate directions and yet hold the poem together as a unit. Here is the complete poem.

Thus it is.
There is much loneliness
and the cigarette coupons will not save us.

I have studied your face across the draughtsboard.
It is freckled and young.
Death and summer have such fine breasts.

Tanned, they return from the sea
The colour of sand, their blouses the colour of waves,
they walk in the large screen of my window.

Bacon, whose Pope screams in the regalia
of chairs and glass, dwarf of all the ages,
an hour-glass of ancient Latin,

you have fixed us where we are, cacti able to talk,
twitched by unintelligible tornadoes,
snakes of collapsing sand.

They trail home from the seaside in their loose blouses.
The idiot bounces his ball as they pass.
He tests his senile smile.[12]

It is common for the opening lines of a Crichton Smith poem to give us the impression that we have just come in on a deliberation which has already lasted for some time. The poem opens with a conversational tag, a nod of the head at something which has already been described, and then, with a sigh, we are given the conclusion or "moral" ("there is much loneliness") of the tale we were too late to hear. Between the first and second verses the poem seems to draw a breath and then set off on another tack. The sight of the youthful face across the draughtsboard (the game of black and white) provokes the near-personification of death *and* summer as shapely women—not separate, but together, as if summer (youth, beauty) and death were doppelgangers of each other. The sun-tanned girls coming back from the sea in the third verse are "real" enough, with no explicit hint of death: but after the identification in line 6 we cannot help being aware of "her" presence in the third verse as well. What happens next is totally unexpected—we suddenly veer aside into a graphic description of one of Francis Bacon's papal portraits, the characteristics of which are then, in the fifth verse, viewed as signs of our own general condition. The first line of the last verse returns us, just as abruptly, to the girls coming back from the seaside. But the poem does not rest there: the final two lines veer off at yet another tangent, their rhythm echoing the inane bouncing of the ball, the testing of the smile.

Structurally then the poem is like a triangle of forces, the forces pulling in very different directions yet still in a complicated equilibrium. The connections between the groups of images are not overtly expressed, for to attempt this would have meant sacrificing the effect of their abrupt proximity, would have led to a ruinous diffusion. Looking at the structure in another way we can see the images in pairs—poet and draughts-player; poet and girls; pope (dead image of our living condition) and idiot (living image of a death-in-life condition); pope and girls; idiot and girls, and so on. The permutations are suggested by the way in which pairs are ordered within each other. And on the conceptual level the theme which holds these images together is the very one ("there is much loneliness") which at the beginning of the poem seemed to belong somewhere else. Every image suggests isolation. There is clearly a gulf of time between the poet and his friend across the draughtsboard. There is no contact between the poet and the girls for they are anonymous and are seen through the screen of his window. The pope on the painting is imprisoned in an attitude of tortured impotence, and "we," as interpreted through the imagery of the painting, are twitched by *unintelligible* tornadoes: we may be "able to talk" but the idea of our being cacti almost cancels out the benefit of such a faculty. The idiot is also isolated, engrossed in his meaningless and repetitive activity as the girls pass him by: his smile is not a means of communication but is simply *tested*, it is another twitch, and means as little as the bouncing of the ball.

The short story "The idiot and the professor and some others"[13] should be read alongside "On a Summer's Day" because it shows an interesting working over of some of the images employed and some of the themes implicit in the poem. The first half of the story describes an encounter between the fifty-year-old idiot and a professor: the latter takes part in the dumbshow childish games of the idiot and thus some communication is achieved, at least to the extent that they laugh together. But this brief companionship ends under the gaze of curious bystanders, the "tanned visitors" on their way home from the sea.

They looked happy and tired, having built sandcastles all day. There were countless numbers of them, and they all stopped to look at the idiot. The idiot snatched the recorder from the professor and the professor made a face and stalked off.

The idiot is back in his isolation. The story ends:

. . . The sea bounded against the rocks.

A boy and a girl stood against a tree whose green leaves made their faces green. The boy put his hand around the girl and caressed her buttocks. She caressed the back of his neck. Her eyes closed. A sheep stared at them. In the distance a motor cycle accelerated. High above the brae there was a rubbish dump full of rats and discarded canisters and the dead body of a ewe.

His father took the recorder from the idiot and put it away in a drawer. The idiot made a sound deep in his throat and scratched his crotch.

51

"If only there was some expression on your face," said the father. "Even one bit of damned expression. Just one iota."

The boy and the girl are in communication with each other, again without words: yet their actions are described in the same mechanical way as the actions of the idiot and the professor. The dead sheep (again!) will be noticed. And of course the idiot's isolation is confirmed by the attitude of his father, in obvious contrast to the behaviour of the professor. Not that the latter is necessarily acting out of understanding or compassion, for we are given to understand that he too is acting out of loneliness.

II

The characteristics of Crichton Smith's imagery which I have described determine the extent to which he can realise his habitual themes as poetry. Those themes are powerfully felt and their recurring presence in his work as a whole give it a strong impression of substance, of pressure, of anxiety to say something that matters. But of course there is a difference between *making remarks* (which may or may not be true, interesting, revealing, etc) and *making poetry*. And in Crichton Smith's case the difference can be described in these terms.—When the imagery exists predominantly for the sake of the theme, for the sake of abstractable thematic content, the imagery has to that extent a diminishing function. From the moment we have fully understood its purpose on an intellectual level and have got the message, the imagery has lost its effect on us: it has served to make a point (e.g. to enliven a remark) and it is conceivable that exactly the same point could have been made in different words. On the other hand when the imagery (the sum or combination of individual images) cannot predominantly be accounted for in terms of thematic content which can be abstracted and discussed, the imagery retains its effect on us and this effect is more than the sum of all the possible explications we may devise. In this case it is inconceivable that exactly the same effect could have been achieved in any other way.

For purposes of discussion the general themes of Crichton Smith's poetry may be roughly separated into four general areas:

(1) social criticism, ranging from small-town *mores* to world events;

(2) the ambivalent qualities of power, will and intelligence;

(3) the language and identity of his own Gaelic background;

(4) loneliness, death, the hard honesty of facing these and the inadequacy of our defences.

It is in the first area, that of social criticism, in which the failure rate is highest, and the weakness is often at two levels: in terms both of what is said (e.g. inadequately considered remarks) and of imagery which fails to operate on more than one plane. Too often the criticism begs questions and aims its points not at any society of living people but at caricatures which have been set up in order to be knocked down. The targets, generally, may be worthy enough: the repressions and monotonies of small-town and suburban life, the mediocrity and fear of excellence in a comfortable society, the cowering hypocrisies of a debased presbyterianism, and so on. But there is little cogency in criticism whose selection of detail is tendentious. In the poem "Scotland"[14] for instance, despite the enumeration, the blows are soft:

> Your artists cower in their walls of stone.
> Apologetic tellers count their notes.
> See on your hills the golfing provosts play.

The poem ends:

> Europe has forgotten you. What are you?
> You are a silence, you're a mineral
> sleep of the dead strata, step on step,
> a house of echoes on a posthumous green.

Gestures as wide as this may include almost everything, or almost nothing.

Crichton Smith's most sustained and explicit attempt at social criticism is the sequence *From Bourgeois Land*[15]. The title, the ordering of some of the poems and much of their content indicate a clear attempt to take a stance and offer direct criticism. But the facile reliance on the epithet "bourgeois," the lack of definition in what is criticised (e.g. the vague connections assumed between capitalism, fascism and presbyterianism), and the relative naivety of the alternative view of life that seems to be proposed (e.g. the pleas for spontaneity in Nos. 30 and 39), all conspire to weaken the book severely as social criticism. Considered as poetry the book is most successful when the general scheme is least observed, in poems whose energy is greater than that needed simply to fulfil the plan. This is particularly so in the case of several poems in which the basic images of the sequence recur—polished spoons, mirrors. watches. In No. 6 ("Hamlet"):

> Images bounce madly against reason
> as in a spoon, wide pictures, fat and jolly.

In No. 11 the "spoon-faced jokes," like the distortions in the hall of mirrors, help to drive the sufferers mad. Then in No. 17 the spoon becomes a kind of crystal ball:

> The wind roars. Thousands of miles it came
> from Biafra or Vietman. I lift my spoon
> and see in it faces without hope or name.

Then there is the watch. In No. 16 ("Church") the small businessmen whose religion is on a par with their trade rest assured in their God

> holy and perfect and invisible
> and punctual as the watch that lies obscured
>
> in an ironed waistcoat on its golden chain
> ticking so comfortably, taking no queer leaps . . .

In No. 25 the retiring employee is presented with a "ponderous watch that holds a soundless scream," i.e. with a cruel reminder that his time is nearly spent. He offers his employers in return "the howling faces of eternity." Then in No. 34 one of the most beautiful images in the book brings together the new space age and the medieval universe and refers to a measure of excellence which perhaps is the real alternative to the mediocre forms of living which are so strenuously rejected:

> Over terraced houses
> these satellites rotate and in deep spaces
> the hammered poetry of Dante turns
> light as a wristwatch, bright as a thousand suns.

*　*　*

No. 27 of *From Bourgeois Land,* whose first three verses are predictable and inauspicious, suddenly generates an interesting complexity towards the end:

> In the underwater light of Sunday School
> only the pale and moderate are lessoned
>
> and then go off to war with faint bowed heads.
> In barbarous sunlight, crops swinging from hands,
> the helmet-headed dazzling riders go
> while clerkish conscripts and their holy brides
> chatter their Yesses from a deeper No.

The attitude towards the pale and moderate ones is plain enough but the attitude towards the dazzling riders is more ambiguous and leads us to the next general group of themes: these concern various aspects of power, the clean decisive characteristics of "those who act," either through will or through intelligence.

The simplest treatments of such themes verge on the simplistic, especially when our admiration is invited for the active. In the sequence "World War One"[16] the fate of Haig trapped in a stony public prison (his reputation) is contrasted with that of the soldiers at the front:

> . . . these men splashing into roses
> through clotting mud, privates mostly
> die into the sentiment of freedom . . .

Those who "died into the freedom of their legend " who "haven't lived/except as heroes who redeemed the world " bear "our hardest envy." One would have thought *that* kind of sentiment had died out of British verse for ever after the poetry that came out of actual experience of the front. More ambiguous treatments of the theme are more honest as when in "The Swan"[17] he declares:

Much that I love is complex and modern. But also
I envy the simple and terrible beaks that they had,
those heroes who stride in progression through poems and vases.

Or when, in "Supposing,"[18] we are asked to imagine a black flower with a brilliantly white interior, a cloud with an intense sun inside it, and a man who experiences a kind of ecstatic warmth

55

inside the suffering that encloses him. The "moral" that follows—
"So, humility moves"—seems to confirm this pattern of what is
positive and good existing within what is negative and evil, but the
image presented in the closing lines disturbs this pattern:

> Great power's like that,
> a wolf in sheep's clothing,
> action inside thought.

In such a context it is natural to find the intellect habitually
regarded with fear and enmity. In an earlier poem on Kierkegaard[19]
we have an extreme example in

> that crucial
> omnivorous intelligence so cruel
> it mocked the pain that made the bare brain howl.

In "The Moon"[20] we find a connection between the moon-image
(with its echoes of virginity, coldness, distance) and the ruthless
efficiency of the intelligence:

> It looked upon Oedipus and taught him how
> the intellect should investigate the flesh,
> the rustlings in the shrubbery . . .

> . . . It is the eye
> of Sir Apollo, the clear operator,
> doctor and sun-god, of the theatre
> the radiant master, scooping out the eyes.

Then from there it is a short step to the cruelty of God (the
supreme intellect), powerfully suggested by the image of electricity
in "Good and Evil"[21]—

> Electricity is waiting in the house.
> I enter it from the snowstorm. I switch on
> the bulb that glows above my battlefield.
> The furniture springs quite clear as we spring clear
> from the dreadful dark of strata, murderous pools.
> God switched it on and suddenly we shook
> in bald vibrations in that merciless light.

Here we have God as a force impinging on us from outside ourselves;

in "Hear us O Lord"[22] God's aggressiveness is seen as an extension of our own admiration for those who are strong, of our own ferocious natures. This is God not so much as the supreme intellect as the supreme criminal:

> Hear us, O Lord, aggression is part of us.
> You polish your jewellery in the salons of heaven.
> Everything about you glitters, your wrist-watch, the diamond
> at your invisible breast, below your invisible beard . . .
>
> . . . As you polish your nails we begin to hate you . . .
>
> . . . You watch us with interest, a glass of pale wine in your hand . . .

This is *our* God, we have created him—"we keep you alive in the silence."

This complex of themes is explored in two of Crichton Smith's most extended poems, "Deer on the High Hills" and "She Teaches Lear." The first of these,[23] called a "meditation," is a sequence of fourteen poems and pays homage to Duncan Ban McIntyre both explicitly (in No. VI) and implicitly, the very difference between the two poets accentuated by their sharing of a common landscape. The structure of the sequence is loose enough to allow the individual poems to catch the shifting connotations of their recurrent images, some of which would undoubtedly be lost with a higher degree of over-all organisation.[24] Thus, the deer exhibit "an inhuman pride;" they stare at us out of an "arrogant atmosphere;" they are aristocratic/noble/royal; they are "balanced on delicate logic" yet move "with great bounding leaps like the mind of God." (No.II). They are "stylish" and their leaps are "unpredictable." (No. V). They "inhabit wild systems" and their violence is motivated not by evil but by desire, by "a running natural lustre"—

> . . . Evil's more complex, is
> a languaged metaphor, like the mists that scarf
> the deadly hind and her bewildered calf.

Though godlike they are vulnerable, "their balance being precarious" (No. VIII). Their "absolute heads" are like "daring thought," half in this world and half out of it; their heads symbolise both a "thirsty intellect" and sensuousness; their air is "imperial" around their "pointed scrutiny, passionate with power." (No. IX). They live on the high peaks, far above the "rampant egos" and the "contorted selves of the plains." (No. XI). They live in a "halfway kingdom," become a "royalty," possess a grace "not theological but of accomplished bodies." (No. XII).

The virtue of the sequence (and others like it) lies in this speculative openness, this leisurely turning of images like crystals, to let different facets catch the light. The potential weaknesses (fragmentation, repetitiveness, contradiction) are obvious—to change the metaphor, the energy of the images can easily be short-circuited like an electric current without enough work to do. "She Teaches Lear"[25] is a very different kind of poem: a single, highly integrated work of 78 lines. While the luminous imagery of "Deer on the High Hills" serves a basically speculative purpose, the speculative elements here are firmly rooted to the individual human predicament of the narrator. Her home life with an ageing and ill father, "a dreadful bitter man" who "hates all life, yet lives," gives her a hard-won understanding of Lear and his relations with his daughters. Her understanding is beyond the reach of most of her pupils, whose responses to Lear's predicament are honest but callow. Their judgments are "cool" and "deadly," their admiration is for

> the absolute hunters, Goneril and Regan,

> beautiful too with their own spare beauty
> when one forgets the haunted piteous fox
> (there's always a fox whenever such ride by).

Understanding them in their innocence of need, she has earned a maturity which brings not only such understanding but also fear of the cruelty of that innocence. The statement with which the poem ends has been wholly earned, and embodies a qualification absent from many of Crichton Smith's shorter poems on a similar theme:

> From our own weakness only are we kind.
> Admire such ones but know in your own mind
> how they would bring upon us innocent carnage,
> the end of Lear, and *Lear*, their own worse will.

* * *

The admiration occasionally expressed in Crichton Smith's poetry (with or without qualification) for vigorous or even violent action tends to be directed towards historically distant archetypes,

58

such as Greek heroes, Roman soldiers, Shakespeare characters, Covenanters, and so on. The *results* of violent action in the contemporary world are regarded more nervously, though here too there is a tendency to rely on a few archetypal examples, as if it were sufficient to *refer* merely to Hiroshima and Nagasaki. The most effective use is made of such references however when they are related to the poet's local background and to his realisation of a common guilt and responsibility.

The television poem "Light to Light"[26] presented these themes very explicitly, in terms of the historical journey from the "green light" which was "nourished" by the monks in their cells on Iona to the "dazzle of blue" over Hiroshima and Nagasaki—the point being that now in *Holy* Loch we have the US Polaris base,

> . . . the Holy Loch
> where our American ships
> guard that civilisation
> which goes on and off like a Belisha beacon,
> precarious, delicate.

The treatment of this theme in some of the Gaelic poems is more personally orientated, as in "A' Dol Dhachaidh" (Going Home).[27] "Tomorrow I will go home to my island," he says, "trying to put a world into forgetfulness." Lewis will be a refuge and there he will rediscover a comforting order, a predictable security. "A dawn or two will rise. A boat will be lying in the glitter of the western sun and water will be running through the world of the similes of my intelligence." Yet he also knows he will take back with him a knowledge that cannot be forgotten, and with that knowledge, guilt. "But I will be thinking (in spite of that) of the great fire that is behind our thoughts, Nagasaki and Hiroshima, and I will hear in a room by myself a ghost or two constantly moving. The ghost of every error, the ghost of every guilt, the ghost of each time I walked past the wounded man on the stony road." Lewis is then not simply an ark of refuge, as in his expectation, but is an ark perilously adrift, "an ark rising and falling on a great sea and no-one knowing whether the dove will ever return, and people talking and talking to each other, and the rainbow of forgiveness in their tears."

Crichton Smith's allegiance to his geographical roots is of course inseparable from his feelings about the Gaelic language, and

59

while the bulk of his poetry is written in English the fact of his bilingualism should not be forgotten. He describes his dilemma in a short Gaelic poem called "The Fool"—

In the dress of the fool, the two colours that have tormented me— English and Gaelic, black and red, the court of injustice, the reason for my anger, and that fine rain from the mountains and those grievous storms from my mind streaming the two colours together so that I will go with poor sight in the one colour that is so odd that the King himself will not understand my conversation.[28]

The defensive position into which Gaelic culture has been forced by all kinds of pressure—economic, political, educational—makes a certain nostalgia inevitable in modern Gaelic writing, though in its finer expressions this nostalgia is very clear-headed and acts as a positive stimulus in the effort to define the difficulties of inhabiting a world ambiguously between two traditions.[29]

"Culture" in the narrower sense is a sensitive register of the condition of the society as a whole. In "Gaelic Songs"[30] the poet, listening to Gaelic songs on the radio, imagines the actualities of the daily life out of which the songs grew, but concludes:

Now they are made of crystal
taking just a moment
between two programmes
elbowing them fiercely
between two darknesses.

But the threat of corruption and extinction comes not only from without, from dominant neighbouring societies, but also from within, from the partial acceptance by highlanders of the fake traditions assigned to them, e.g. in the name of tourism. "At the Highland Games"[31] is a hurt and angry poem whose feelings are too hard to be described as nostalgic: the references like that to "the pibroch stirring my consciousness like a breeze a loch" carry not so much despair for an excellence in danger of being lost as contempt for shoddy alternatives. The poem ends:

Finished. All of it's finished. The Gaelic
boils in my mouth, the South Sea silver stick

60

twirls, settles. The mannequins are here.
Calum, how you'd talk of their glassy stare,

their loud public voices. Stained pictures
of what was raw, violent, alive and coarse.

I watch their heirs, Caligulas with canes
stalk in their rainbow kilts towards the dance.

Yet, however painful, the allegiance is inescapable, in terms not of
tragedy and imprisonment but of a renewable sense of belonging and
acceptance. "To have found one's own country" is like having
endured a long journey or pilgrimage only to discover that it was
"around one all the time."

> To have fallen in love with
> stone, thistle and strath,
> to see the blood flow
> in wandering old rivers,
> this wound is not stanched
> by handkerchiefs or verse.
> This wound was after all
> love and a deep curse. [32]

Several of these related themes, especially the idea of the uniqueness of a language to the people who use it to define both their own
identity and their view of the world, are gathered in the 25-part
Gaelic poem "Am Faigh A' Ghàidhlig Bàs?" (Shall Gaelic Die?). [33]
The loose structure of the sequence, of a type we have already noted
in other sequences, allows considerable speculative freedom, yet the
speculation is anchored to very particular and concrete images as in
the following three extracts:

13

Were you ever in a maze? Its language fits your language. Its
roads fit the roads of your head. If you cannot get out of the
language you cannot get out of the maze. Its roads reflect your
language. O for a higher language, like a hawk in the sky, that
can see the roads, that can see their end, like God who built the
roads, our General Wade. The roads of the Highlands fit the
roads of our language.

21

God is outside language, standing on a perch. He crows now and again. Who hears him? If there is a God let him emanate from the language, a perfume emanating from the dew of the morning, from the various-coloured flowers.

25

The gold is new. It will not rust. "Immutable, universal," as the Frenchman said. But the pennies, the pounds, the half-crowns, these coins that are old and dirty, the notes that are wrinkled like old faces, they are coping with time, to these I give my allegiance, to these I owe honour, with sweetness. "Immutable, perfect," Midas with his coat of gold and of death.

* * *

The complexes of themes I have so far distinguished occur throughout Crichton Smith's work. The fourth group of themes—loneliness, the facing of death, exposure to raw experience, the frailty of poetry and our other defences—I have left to the last because although these do occur in earlier work they have recently become more dominant.

Loneliness is most often seen in terms of those defences which people erect to protect their vulnerability, not only from others but also from their own self-awareness, as in "Jean Brodie's Children"—

> Mistresses, iron in their certainty,
> their language unambiguous but their lives
> trembling on grey boughs.[34]

Or in the first poem of "By the Sea," where the poet looks to his own possible defences:

> I lock my will
> on the National Health Service, will not fall
>
> too deep for rescue but for the mind, the mind.

and at others';

> Thick rings
>
> of routine save us, rings like marriage rings.
> The yachts seem free in their majestic goings

and the great ships at rest. Helmeted girls
emerge from salons with their golden curls.[35]

The extreme of loneliness, the facing of death, has also been a recurring theme, though with a notable sharpening of focus in the later
work. If we look at the beautifully modulated closing lines of one of
his best known earlier poems, "Old Woman"[36]—

> And nothing moved within the knotted head
>
> but only a few poor veins as one might see
> vague wishless seaweed floating on a tide
> of all the salty waters where had died
> too many waves to mark two more or three.

—if we look at these lines we can sense a distinct confidence in the
verse, in its powers to articulate gracefully and thereby to move us.
More recent treatments of such themes show a greater nervousness,
a starker realisation that any defences we put up, poetic, religious,
technological, are desperately frail. Compare "Old Woman" with
the poem beginning "You told me once how your younger brother
died,"[37] in which the poet recalls how the drowning man sang a
psalm to bring his rescuers near, but in vain.

> You died of lack of oxygen. I tried
> to fit the mask against your restless face
> in the bumpy ambulance in which you lay.
> I thought that moment of the psalm as guide,
> beyond our vain technology, the grey
> and scarlet blankets which you tossed aside.

Such a tendency is admitted in the closing remarks of a recent
interview:

Interviewer: *Stand* magazine has now published a number of
poems on death. Is your course becoming circular, and will the
years ahead be difficult ones?
I.C.S.: Oh, I think they will be difficult ones because I think,
really, that everything I have ever done is really eventually
coming to this question. What is death? What is a dead person,
and in the end what is the value of writing when one is confronted
by a dead person?[38]

63

It would be a mistake, I believe, to regard this as a poetic impasse. No doubt,

> If you are about to die now
> there is nothing I can write for you,[39]

but it is as well to remember Crichton Smith's belief that it is part of the function of poetry to face such apparently insurmountable facts of experience, even if the poetry fails in the attempt. The importance of feeling exposed—

> To have felt everything so intensely
> is like skin after skin peeling off[40]

—and the low value he places on poetry which does not try to meet new, raw experience are key elements in his thinking about poetry:

> You see, I believe that the greatest poetry is created at the moment when you are at the frontiers. That is to say, when you are absorbing and transforming new material, that is, material which hasn't been transformed before. Now that is why I think Robert Lowell is a very great poet, because he is transforming raw material.[41]

Of course this entails scepticism of any prop or achievement that may tempt us, but the scepticism is not absolute: it too may be just a prop. Certainly, if it were absolute the poetry would never get written.

> I freely admit my imagination's stained
> by that hard world, composed of stone and wind,
> men in black hats, and women in black scarves,
> the broken fences and the broken wharves,
> a world of gorse and mountains, bibles, streams,
> ceilidhs and dances, moonlight and bad dreams,
> world without theatre or gallery,
> merely the changing drama of the sky,
> artless, without art. And sometimes I
> believe I do not care for poetry,
> I mean deep down, where our decisions lie,
> sharks and pale monsters, for I know the sea,
> its glittering surface, but below there blows
> not Free Church poetry but bad Free Church prose.[42]

Notes

S.P.—*Selected Poems* (Gollancz, 1970).

H.A.—*Hamlet in Autumn* (Lines Review Editions No. 2, 1972).

Where translations of Gaelic poetry are given, these are by I. C. S. himself.

1. Review of Maurice Lindsay's *This Business of Living* in *Akros*, July 1969.
2. *The Golden Lyric* (Akros Publications, 1967). Cf. similar image in *S.P.*, p. 40.
3. *L.R. 29* (June, 1969), p. 28.
4. *S.P.*, p. 93.
5. *The Last Summer* (Gollancz, 1969), p. 35. See also *H.A.*, p. 60, "Everything is Silent."
6. *L.R. 29*, p. 3.
7. *S.P.*, pp 17–18. First collected in *Thistles and Roses* (Eyre and Spottiswoode, 1961).
8. *Consider the Lilies* (Gollancz, 1968), pp 98–99. Cf. the juxtaposition of the whiteness of a dead gull and the whiteness of the girl's dress in "By Ferry to the Islands," *S.P.*, p. 20.
9. p. 108. The hallway of Strathnaver Manse (p. 100) recurs in *From Bourgeois Land*, No. 2.
10. *S.I.R.*, May 1970, p. 10.
11. *S.I.R.*, September 1971, p. 24.
12. *H.A.*, p. 7. See also the reference to Bacon in "Party," *H.A.*, p. 27.
13. *Survival without Error* (Gollancz, 1970), pp 221–23. Cf. "Russian Poem," 8, *H.A.*, p. 22.
14. *S.I.R.*, August 1968, p. 22.
15. Gollancz, 1969. In his review of the book in *L.R. 29* John MacQueen usefully suggests some thematic parallels with *Consider the Lilies*.
16. *S.P.*, pp 45–51. Cf. "Poem," *L.R. 28* (March, 1969), p. 15—
    > Better the headlong soldier in his wrath
    > than the cool hand that plotted his hot graph.
17. *L.R. 28*, p. 14.
18. *L.R. 24* (June, 1967), p. 8.
19. *S.P.*, p. 19. First collected in *Thistles and Roses*.
20. *H.A.*, p. 8. Some of this imagery is developed further in another fine recent poem, "Oedipus and Others" *H.A.*, p. 9, beginning:
    > The god Apollo scratched out both his eyes.
    > Tragedy is light too bright to bear.
    > There were no choices in that azure heaven
    > no mercy, only justice . . .
21. *H.A.*, p. 10.
22. *S.P.*, p. 94.
23. *S.P.*, pp 27–41, first published as a pamphlet by Giles Gordon in 1962. I. C. S.'s translation of Duncan Ban McIntyre's "Ben Dorain" appeared from Akros Publications in 1969.

24. Cf. the comparable structure of the sequences "By the Sea," *S.P.*, pp 79–89; "Transparencies," *L.R. 29*, pp 20–32; "Shall Gaelic Die?" *S.P.*, pp 103–110; and "The White Air of March," *S.I.R.*, August 1969, pp 28–34.

25. *S.P.*, pp 67–69.

26. The concluding passages were printed in *L.R. 26* (June 1968), pp 9–11.

27. *H.A.*, p. 40. It is worth pointing out that an overt treatment of the contemporary world at large was foreign to modern Gaelic poetry until Sorley Maclean broke the boundaries with *Dain do Eimhir* (1943). I. C. S.'s translation of a large part of this book was published by Gollancz and Northern House (Newcastle) in 1971.

28. *H.A.*, p. 41.

29. See for instance the poetry of Derick Thomson, discussed in chapter four.

30. *H.A.*, p. 42.

31. *S.P.*, p. 75. These themes are developed in the 16-poem sequence "The White Air of March," *S.I.R.*, August 1969, e.g. the admirable daring of writers and thinkers who did take risks (No. 7), the loneliness of being an exile in one's own land (No. 8), tourism as the shabby diminishment of a way of life (No. 12), excellence as a warning and a challenge (the recurrent image of the Cuillins).

32. "To have found one's own country," *L.R. 28*, p. 16. Cf. "Home," *S.P.*, p. 23.

33. Gaelic and English in *L.R. 29*, pp 33–45; English alone in *S.P.*, pp 103–110.

34. *S.P.*, p. 97.

35. *S.P.*, p. 79. Cf. part 4 of "In the Cafe," where the social observation is as sharp as any in *From Bourgeois Land* but the informing spirit is compassion rather than anger.

36. *S.P.*, p. 15. First collected in *Thistles and Roses*.

37. *Love Poems and Elegies* (Gollancz, 1972), p. 14.

38. *S.I.R.*, September 1971, p. 27.

39. *S.P.*, p. 99.

40. "Three Poems for Christmas," *L.R. 28*, p. 11.

41. *S.I.R.*, May 1970, p. 10.

42. Lines from unpublished work, 1971.

III

NORMAN MacCAIG

NORMAN MacCAIG's first publications appeared in the 1940's: he contributed nine poems to *The White Horseman*, edited by J. F. Hendry and Henry Treece, in 1941, and then had two collections of his own published, *Far Cry* (Routledge, 1943) and *The Inward Eye* (Routledge, 1947). It is doubtful if the so-called apocalyptic movement in British poetry would bear much examination now, though if we look at it as a social and not just as a literary phenomenon it does throw some light on the role which many poets in the forties assumed. In view of the kind of audience they evidently wrote for, and the manner in which they set about reaching it, their accepted role must have been a marginal one. Could such poetry, with its tortured syntax and private imagery, survive the kind of exposure to which much contemporary poetry is now subjected by way of live readings? Were these poets at all interested in this kind of accessibility?

The fact that MacCaig included none of this work in his *Selected Poems* (1971) confirms his rejection of everything he wrote before the age of 37, and it is fair to regard his main published work as beginning with *Riding Lights* (1955). Yet it is interesting to note that the break was not absolute, for there are several themes, turns of phrase even, in the earlier work which we recognise through our familiarity with their later appearances. Here for instance is Poem No. 13 from *Far Cry*:

Here I stumble, on the fingernail size of a minute
or the leafy plates of hours, hemlock on hemlock
that choke my mincing river, tangle my plummet.
Time smiles in the corner, holding diplomatic gifts
wrapped in fine language and his immensely jewelled stick
at the same time thrust between ankles. In my loft

I see the wide spaces reserved and cobwebby with images
to receive the sturdy harvest that outside the sun
is shrivelling away, the same sun that rummages
in the dusty furniture of my mind; and so leaves me
with ghost corn in the field and an empty barn,
and I sitting spiritless, a tick-tocking shadow.

In No. 18 we find some characteristic play on the idea of metaphor:

Beauty of yours clouds any fire
and makes a lie of all my metaphor . . .

So dispossessed I cry
old kingdoms in my darkness,
and greet with my clapping cock-crow
the colours
you cloud so with your other fire
that burns me into metaphor.

And in No. 25 we find this image—

. . . and my portcullis eye
opens and swarms with their thousand midget spies
each with a swagbag world swayed on his shoulders.

—which could well remind us of "Instrument and Agent," the
opening poem of *Riding Lights.*

And while we can make such references forward from the forties
to the fifties, we can also make a few references back, particularly
from some of the poems in *The Sinai Sort* (1957), whose first poem,
"A Man in the Seed," contains the stanza:

And dark in my sometimes self I take the dark
Close to my famished breast where worlds of weeping
Slide their sad stars down twinkling in daylight.
My hands are shafts of shadows, my nails are night,
And round these bones, my frail and songless ark,
My arms are crooked with their crooked keeping.

Yet if the break between the forties and the fifties is not absolute
then it is certainly startling. *Far Cry* and *The Inward Eye* were
after all the work of a man over thirty and one could have expected
subsequent work to show a close continuity of development. *Riding
Lights*, however, published when MacCaig was forty-five, shows a
remarkably altered style and tone: this poetry communicates far
beyond the capacities of the earlier idiom. Whether one regards
this as a late start, or as a fresh start after a false one, hardly matters. [1]

* * *

The opening lines in *Riding Lights*—

In my eye I've no apple; every object
Enters in there with hands in pockets

—herald one of the strongest interests in MacCaig's poetry: the

70

enigmatic relations between observer and observed. The landscape
or the person we observe, and the mind which thinks it sees and
knows, are linked by that deceitful lens, the eye.

> All that the eye names is disguises.
> That's no tree but a way of feeling.
>
> ("Lies for Comfort," S.S., p. 8)

Mind and eye, seer and seen, name and thing, disguise and reality,
fiction and stony fact—all are in a constant *process* of interaction,
like the changing partners in a complicated endless dance figure.
Since the eye keeps open house, as it were, so the mind is equally
accommodating, whether the guests can be described as "real"
or not. "Perfect Morning" (M., p. 19) for instance, ends:

> . . . having nowhere to disperse
>
> Its secret selves, even the unreal
> Emerged and took its real place,
> With civil looks admitting all
> The actual world into its grace.

Indeed, the very deceits of appearance, the fictions in which reality
presents itself, are indispensable to our modes of knowing. In
"Particular You" (S.S., p. 12) the poet says

> Reveal to me no more
> Than what I know of you—your bright disguises . . .

because

> . . . the language of disguise
> Says all I want and bear to know.

Even the shape a man has may be "lies to let us know him" ("Inverkirkaig Bay," C.G., p. 34).

Mind and eye of course are not passive: they relate to the outside
world in an intricate pattern of defence and aggression. They
select, destroy, create. They can stare a landscape out of existence.[2]
In "Birds all Singing" (R.L., p. 48) their activity is parallelled to
the sweet/violent ambiguity of bird-song. The man, the perceiver
and mythmaker, sees a bird which in its own way is also a perceiver
and mythmaker. Birds, we are told, sing not for sweetness or love
but for the sake of asserting territorial claims:

71

Not passion but possession. A miserly
Self-enlargement that muddles mine and me
Says the half-acre is the bird, and he,
Deluded to that grandeur, swells, and with
A jolly roundelay
Of boasts and curses establishes a myth.

The human listens and "feels it innocent, calls it pastoral," yet if he is deceived by the bird, he is equally deceiving himself:

So he, his own enlargement also, thinks
A quiet thought in his corner that creates
Territories of existence, private states
Of being where trespassers are shot at sight;
And myth within myth blinks
Its blind eyes on the casual morning light.

For the poet, the inescapable bond between experience and reflection, between "a squelching countryside" and "a dry thought," is metaphor.[3] Here, too, we find not simple correspondences but ever-changing permutations. The effort to comprehend, for instance, may simply open a series of mysteries, as in "Ego" (S.S., p. 32, S.P., p. 30):

. . . Tree
And star are ways of finding out what I
Mean in a text composed of earth and sky.

What reason to believe this, any more
Than that I am myself a metaphor
That's noticed in the researches of a rose
And self-instructs a star? . . .

If time keeps on destroying the evidence, the researcher will succeed only in discovering more secrets. Likeness may be unstable, and the point of a true comparison may recede indefinitely, as in "Non Pareil" (S.S., p. 50):

A ship sails clean out of its mataphor
And birds perch on no simile . . .

. . . You and all
The likenesses my greedy mind commits
To help its exploration of you are
As different as a slow-worm and a star.

72

Hence the *thingness* of a thing, or the indefinable uniqueness of a person, may remain inaccessible behind or beyond whatever models/symbols/identities we may devise as traps.

> Even a leaf, its own shape in the air,
> Achieves its mystery not by being symbol
> Or ominous of anything but what it is . . .
>
>   ("Two Ways of It," C.G., p. 32, S.P., p. 44)

The mind's apparent inability to see things "as they are" is an obvious function of its creative power, of its power to select, reject and interpret its evidence. The point is neatly made, by way of a complaint *against* this power, in "Humanism" (S., p. 8). If we think of one of the glaciers which, as it melted, carved the landscape of the North West Highlands, we may imagine it as a retreating army:

> What a human lie is this. What greed and what
> Arrogance, not to allow
> A glacier to be a glacier—
> To humanise into a metaphor
> That long slither of ice . . .
>
> I defend the glacier that
> When it absorbs a man
> Preserves his image
> Intact.

Again, the final poem in *Rings on a Tree*, "No Choice" (p. 62), alternates an explicit weariness with metaphor with a demonstration of how nevertheless metaphor cannot be avoided. The poem begins

> I think about you
> in as many ways as rain comes . . .

but then interrupts itself:

> (I am growing, as I get older,
> to hate metaphors—their exactness
> and their inadequacy.)

Yet the comparison in the first two lines is developed metaphorically:

73

these thoughts ("about you") are sometimes "a moistness," sometimes "a rattling shower," sometimes "a drowning downpour." The poem ends by returning to the inadequacy of metaphors, but without the parentheses:

> I am growing, as I get older,
> to hate metaphor,
> to love gentleness,
> to fear downpours.

But how does one express a love of gentleness or a fear of downpours other than by metaphor? There is, it seems, no choice.

* * *

These points which I have abstracted and summarised indicate the kind of interests we find in a large part of MacCaig's work, and at their best the poems which fall into this first grouping partake themselves of the sleight-of-hand of perception. The poems present themselves as elegant performances, very conscious of *being* aware and very curious about *how* they are aware, and often half-concealing half-revealing a deadly sincerity behind the most playful conceits. The enigma of simple objects ("Lighthouse," R.A., p. 16, S.P., p. 56; "Things in Each Other," R.A., p. 28, S.P., p. 54) becomes an enigma within a mystery when the object contemplated is also a person ("Two Ways of It," C.G., p. 32, S.P., p. 44; "True Ways of Knowing," M., p. 55, S.P., p. 76), but the resultant sense of revelation can at times be surprisingly uncomplicated.

The speculative element in this poetry is most productive when the focus on the observed object is sharpest—despite a clear attraction for the poetry of Wallace Stevens, MacCaig does not seem to share Stevens' interest in abstract speculation as such. When the focus occasionally blurs the poetry too is blurred, abstracting rather than defining, and an unbridgeable gap widens between observation and reflection. "July Evening" (R.A., p. 54), for instance, opens with three neat miniatures:

> A bird's voice chinks and tinkles
> Alone in the gaunt reedbed—
> Tiny silversmith
> Working late in the evening.

74

I sit and listen. The rooftop
With a quill of smoke stuck in it
    Wavers against the sky
In the dreamy heat of summer.

Flowers' closing time: bee lurches
Across the hayfield, singing
    And feeling its drunken way
Round the air's invisible corners.

But now the poet simply shuts his eyes and forgets what he has seen:

And grass is grace. And charlock
Is gold of its own bounty.
    The broken chair by the wall
Is all of immortal landscapes.

Something has been completed
That everything is part of,
    Something that will go on
Being completed forever.

The abstractions of "grace," "bounty" and "immortal landscapes"
are merely asserted, unearned by the poem, and in the last verse we
have to be content with the vaguest of all: "something."[4] Another
aspect of this occasional lack of focus can be seen in the last verse
of "Country Morning" (S.S., p. 55):

Measuring this with what remains of my
Failure to measure it is what enables
Such self-dividing statement as this is.
I throw such measurement away, and as it dwindles
Into myself, my speech ends and I lean
On the door that opens on what myself can mean.

The word "what" in the first, second and sixth lines here is used
merely as a kind of pivot to help the writer over into the next phrase:
just *what* the "what" is, is seldom defined, and the riddle turns
back on itself. There are several examples in *Riding Lights*,[5] but in
The Sinai Sort, MacCaig at his most riddling, this type of construction seems habitual.[6] Thereafter it vanishes almost entirely. A
similar though much less frequent construction, using "more"/"less"

75

is worth noting in passing—for instance, "Inverkirkaig Bay"
(C.G., p. 34) ends:

> Such clarity of seeming can declare
> More than my utter self to me, who say
> In clouds of words less than that false cloud there.

On occasions like this the reader is left guessing what exactly *is*
"more" or "less."[7]

If the focus blurs, reflection ousts observation, the mind takes
over from the eye. At the other extreme, poetry which narrows its
focus to the point where reflection is excluded suffers from another
kind of restriction—it lacks the movement of the mind beneath
the verse, controlling its purpose. In MacCaig's poetry this can
have the effect of reducing potentially important themes to a level
of decoration or even whimsy, as if the eye playfully distracts the
mind. The metaphors, identities and transformations exist for
their own sake and may even stand at odds with the true progress
of the poem. This may hardly matter if the purpose of the poem
is little more than the statement of a series of identities: "In a Level
Light" (R.A., p. 25, S.P., p. 51), for example, simply parallels a
natural scene with a set of ecclesiastical references (no fewer than
16 of them in 14 lines) without there being any compelling reason
for such references being made in the first place. But it does matter
in the case of a poem like "Sound of the Sea on a Still Evening"
(R.A., p. 9). The first stanza establishes a sense of immanence
without apparently departing from simple meteorological observation:

> It comes through quietness, softly crumbling in
> Till it becomes the quietness; and we know
> The wind to be will reach us from Loch Roe.
> From the receding South it will begin
> To stir, to whisper; and by morning all
> The sea will lounge North, sloping by Clachtoll.

The implications are allowed then to develop, more abstractly in
the second stanza, more concretely in the third, which ends with
the remarkable image:

> An unseen bird goes by,
> Its little feathers hushing the whole sky.

76

The final stanza, however, with its prophecy of next morning's tumult ("pebbles will roar/At their harsh labour"), ends in an example of decorative reduction which runs counter to the purpose which the poem has clearly established.

> . . . and tall waves will run
> Fawning on rocks and barking in the sun.

These doggy waves belong somewhere else (e.g. if a comic reduction were relevant) but not here.

Granted, this decorative element in MacCaig's work is important and accounts, rightly, for much of its popularity. He is a fertile inventor of cameo-type miniatures which are easily remembered and quoted—neat and witty metaphors for water, wind, rock and mist; for animals such as dragon-flies, frogs, grasshoppers, beetles, sheep, mackerel, ravens, bees, gulls, cormorants, stags, pigeons, larks, mice, hornets, hedgehogs and herons; and machines like concrete-mixers.[8] Yet if we look beyond the immediate effect it is clear that this element contributes effectively to any particular poem only when it is fully integrated with the poem's purpose, when the metaphors actively promote the development of the poem. In "Laggandoan, Harris" (R.L., p. 46), for example, the first, second, third and fifth stanzas describe a landscape so full of fanciful transformations that it is toy-like—a dragon-fly "makes a thin/Tottering grass its anchor-post,/Changed to a small blue zeppelin," and a grasshopper "scours/His little pail," and so on. But in the fourth stanza a human appears:

> Down from the moor, between two rocks
> The furnace sun has calcined white,
> Johann, humped with a creel of peats,
> Comes leaning forward through the light.

Unlike the animals, Johann is not transfigured—the only metaphorical element in his description is the possibly ominous "humped." One of the implications then is that the freedom of playful disguise and transformation is an aspect of innocence. There is another interesting example in "Skittles" (M., p. 20, S.P., p. 67). The first two stanzas are playful enough—the ball, "That ought to trundle smooth on its small thunder" becomes first a creature with two legs, one shorter than the other; then a toad, "crippling away;"

then a square. The bottles are brown penguins. The idea that the ball doesn't have much of his intentions left is however developed in the third and final stanza:

> From snake to mantis to man
> I stand upright and turn away. Behind me
> A demolition says my fate has found me.
> My lost intention has done what I once began.

The transformations of the man as he rises from the horizontal to the crouching to the vertical contrast with the transformations of the ball as it becomes less and less like itself. But with their evolutionary suggestion, and linked with the idea of "fate," they serve to open up the implications of the poem. The account of the game may itself be a game yet at the same time a serious business.

The possibilities of this kind of metaphorical facility seem to be most completely realised in poetry of a relatively small scale. Indeed some of MacCaig's most perfectly realised poems rely on a single image, like the tree in "Wet Snow" (R.L., p. 9) or the dripping oars in "Old Man Thinking" (R.T., p. 49), or a pair of similar images, like the two shepherds/poets in "Two Shepherds" (S., p. 49) or the two wells in "The Red Well, Harris" (R.T., p. 43). Clearly this kind of "perfection" becomes less important on a larger scale but it is interesting to note the effect of MacCaig's small-scale propensities on his few longer poems.[9] Despite their considerable interest on other counts, the enclosing and local effect of clear-cut decorative imagery can impede rather than promote the more leisurely, open-ended, forward movement demanded by an extended poem.

* * *

There is another grouping of poems in which the element of performance gains a further interest in that it is accompanied by doubts about itself. In these poems the poet is not only putting on a witty or interesting performance but he is simultaneously standing back and questioning what he is up to. Indeed the apparent confidence of the performance is often in itself an indication of inner hesitancy and self-doubt.

Two very different poems will suggest terms. The first, "Gifts" (S.S., p. 24, S.P., p. 29) opens:

You read the old Irish poet and complain
I do not offer you impossible things—
Gloves of bee's fur, cap of the wren's wings,
Goblets so clear light falls on them like a stain.
I make you the harder offer of all I can,
The good and ill that make of me this man.

This is a very characteristic theme, especially in love poems, and its interest often arises from the fact that this desire to do "impossible" things is frequently irresistible. The other poem is "Frogs" (S., p. 15, S.P., p. 99), which ends:

Above all, I love them because,
Pursued in water, they never
Panic so much that they fail
To make stylish triangles
With their ballet dancer's
Legs.

Now self-understanding, self-doubt, the honesty of recognising one's own good and ill, may well cause a man panic: and the greater the panic, the more stylish his gestures may become. Some of the poet's gestures may have to do with wit—in a poem like "Sense about Nonsense" (S.S., p. 23), which could also be seen as "Nonsense about Sense," the final effect of wit's riddling may be a state of witlessness in the face of "collapsing places/That may be heaven or hell for all you know." Other gestures may have to do with mystical or philosophical perception—as in "Vestey's Well" (M., p. 15) we may try to feel that we are "each one a bright/And delicate place with a philosopher in it," but succeed in seeing not Nothing but nothing. Even the most obvious of the poet's gestures, saying, may be a defensive manner of avoiding reality: one says anything *but* what one knows is the truth, as in "No Nominalist" (S., p. 37, S.P., p. 105) where the refusal to play Adam is a fear of learning "the meaning/Of the snake's hiss."

For more effective illustration two short poems are worth quoting complete. The first is "By a Water" (M.P., p. 36). Here there is an interesting correlation between two sets of metaphors, one (vv. 1, 3) pertaining to the poet's gestures, the other (vv. 2, 4) pertaining to his self-knowledge.

The sky was wet zinc.
Waves snuffled along the low cliffs—
what were they longing to get at?

You spoke words
that turned into wounds. I was guilty
only of being me.

The sky came down on my eyes.
I stared at the world
through a web of zinc.

And inside me something went snuffling,
searching for a victim
to lay at your feet.

The second is "Basking Shark" (M.P., p. 38, S.P., p. 116), more genial but no less serious.

To stub an oar on a rock where none should be,
To have it rise with a slounge out of the sea
Is a thing that happened once (too often) to me.

But not too often—though enough. I count as gain
That once I met, on a sea tin-tacked with rain,
That roomsized monster with a matchbox brain.

He displaced more than water. He shoggled me
Centuries back—this decadent townee
Shook on a wrong branch of his family tree.

Swish up the dirt and, when it settles, a spring
Is all the clearer. I saw me, in one fling,
Emerging from the slime of everything.

So who's the monster? The thought made me grow pale
For twenty seconds while, sail after sail,
The tall fin slid away and then the tail.

The gestures are made with consummate neatness—"slounge," "tin-tacked," and the rhythmical stop-start of lines 3–4. Both monster (1.6) and man (1.8) are deflated. Then lines 10–13 almost make explicit a large and serious theme, i.e. the reversal of man and monster—but not quite, for the gestures in the last two lines once again deflate both man ("For twenty seconds" only, in case he looked like taking himself too earnestly) and monster (the rhyme and rhythm suggesting the almost toylike nature of the disappearing beast).

*   *   *

A third group of poems can be distinguished: those in which the element of performance, regarded either innocently or sceptically, is much less important. The gestures may still be made crisply, but they now aim at a sombre clarity of statement. The distance between writer and reader is closer, allowing a tone which if not exactly confessional at least makes it possible to express doubt and fear more directly. The surface of these poems tends to be relatively calm and transparent, while the undercurrents are often bitter. As for difficulty, the poems of the first two groups may at times be more difficult for the reader, particularly the riddling poetry of *A Sinai Sort*. This third group on the other hand, is generally more accessible, if only up to a point determined by MacCaig's reticence, but may represent a greater difficulty for the writer, in terms of honesty won against odds.

It is not simply a matter of making more explicit statements, for in the small number of poems in which MacCaig has tried to make explicit statements of a more social nature the generality of the statement has tended to dissipate whatever particularity of feeling generated the poems in the first place.[10] Nor is it simply a matter of passing years, for poems of this group occur throughout his work—there are at least half a dozen, for instance, in *Riding Lights*.[11] Indeed it is worth noting how in the *Selected Poems* a relatively high proportion of poems of this kind are retained, at the expense of the first two groupings I suggested. This emphasis is quite marked if the reader approaches the selection with a familiar knowledge of the eight collections (nearly 380 poems) from which it is drawn.

A good initial example of this kind of poem is "Dilemma" (S., p. 26—not in S.P.) because it includes, within the unsolved dilemma, questions about the nature of perception and imagination which are so often the matter of poems in the first two groups.

> I move among sensations
> Like a mist . . .

The mist creates appearances: a loch appears where none should be, a stone is a stag, a cliff is a cloud. The situation is, literally, obscure. But what happens if the obscurity clears?

> If I were completely dispersed,
> Which will happen, will happen . . .

things may indeed appear "as they are"—

> But where would I be
> To notice them? . . . So I'm afraid
> When the sun makes me
> Luminous—I thicken myself against him
> And move disconsolately
> Amongst my gray apparitions
> Till I am my opaquest self, and then,
> What gloom.

On the one hand, the tendency towards clarity and annihilation; on the other, the contrary tendency towards creation and obscurity: and the poet is caught between.

Despite the "I" of the narrator, however, "Dilemma" remains a fairly general statement and on the whole the poems in this group have a more clearly marked personal pressure behind them. This can be felt even in poems where the exact nature of the threat remains undefined and where the experience is distanced into the third person. In "Flooded Mind" (S., p. 38, S.P., p. 102) the flood waters have risen to submerge the entire landscape and although they have now fallen, that landscape will never be the same again:

> No wonder his eyes were
> Noticeboards saying
> *Private. Keep out.*

The poem itself affirms that injunction for despite the clarity with which the metaphor is developed we are given no hint at all as to the nature of the "flood"—we have to accept that it happened without learning any of its circumstances. Equally undefined are the circumstances behind "Spilled Salt" (M.P., p. 32, S.P., p. 125), and the sense of bitter involvement stronger than anywhere else in his work. The salt image obviously carries an allusion to Lot's wife, but the main preparation for the very direct conclusion is by means of some characteristic remarks on the way we measure our

82

human scale against inert natural objects, both large (Suilven) and small (a miniature mountain of spilled salt). The poem ends—

> She whose look
> gave me the size
> I thought I was
>
> became spilled salt;
> for she
> had stopped noticing.
>
> I look at her image.
> I hate it.
> I sweep it away.

The poem as a whole remains enigmatic: for the reader not enough is clarified; for the writer perhaps this is as much as can be clarified.

On the other hand the circumstances in "Visiting Hour" (R.T., p. 21, S.P., p. 80) are much more explicit than usual, and it is interesting to see how the resolution

> I will not feel, I will not
> feel, until
> I have to

is broken, because the feeling is admitted and defined through the careful selection of those circumstances. "Sounds of the Day" (S., p. 19, S.P., p. 100) also admits a recognisable event (a separation) but describes it in terms of shutting a door on all the noises of the outside world, i.e. the world in which the poet discovers his surprising correspondences. In the negation which follows this exclusion:

> I thought I was hurt in my pride only,
> Forgetting that,
> When you plunge your hand in freezing water,
> You feel
> A bangle of ice round your wrist
> Before the whole hand goes numb.

Similarly, in "In my Mind" (M.P., p. 62, S.P., p. 126) the world which the poet inhabits, both physically and imaginatively, is threatened with total exclusion, this time from within itself, from "that terrible cul-de-sac"—

83

> I turn away from
> the smiling house there
>
> and the room in it
> with green blinds drawn
>
> and a bed with a bed lamp shedding
> its kind light down
>
> on a dead hand
> and a book fallen from it.

The house, we notice, is "smiling" and the light is "kind," as if one could walk down the cul-de-sac very easily and unwittingly. Naturally enough, this piece comes at the very end of the *Selected Poems.*

Indeed the last five poems in the selected volume suggest not only the remarkable range that can be traced back through the entire output, but also a general tenor which the selection tends to stress. On the latter point, for instance, it would not have been difficult, quantitatively, to make a selection that was all wit and fireworks. Those last five are:

(1) "Venus Fly-Trap" (love at its most predatory).

(2) "Shifts" (the riddling, fencing aspects of love).

(3) "Walking to Inveruplan" (one of the most genial pieces in the book, the more so because of its placing here).

(4) "Spilled Salt."

(5) "In My Mind."

* * *

The defensive element in MacCaig's work is strong in the sense that when the performance is most skilful the element of personal involvement and exposure is least noticeable: the wit can often be a way of saying "*Private. Keep out,*" a kind of aggressive camouflage. This places him at some distance from the more consistently serious and defenceless manner in which Iain Crichton Smith pursues his obsessions, and also from the openness with which Crichton Smith will talk about his work. At the same time it also places him at some distance, in another direction, from the outgoing curiosity and craftsmanlike skill with which Edwin Morgan responds to such a wide range of stimuli. Indeed if we imagine the substantial body of work now produced by MacCaig, Crichton Smith and Morgan as a kind of triangle of forces, we have a very interesting and variegated series of poetic responses to what in many instances are remarkably similar circumstances, social, geographical and historical.[12]

Naturally enough, poets as such appear in MacCaig's poems. In "A Writer" (S., p. 34) we have a poet (MacDiarmid?) who in the difficult years learned to dodge ("Just as a stoned crow/Invents ways of flying/It had never thought of before") but now when he is flying far beyond the reach of stones, is still prone to lurch and twirl. In "Two Shepherds" (S., p. 49) we have two poets, the Dionysian and the Apollonian, the hectic and the calm, who *both* get their sheep into the fold. In the opening poem of *A Common Grace* ("Creator") we have the poet as nosey-parker, "thrumming at all his nerve-ends." In the opening poem of *Surroundings* ("Metaphysical Me") we have the poet as an "infinite bigamist" who grew bored and wanted to divorce the lot but "found he couldn't/ For the sake of the children." Again, *Rings on a Tree* opens with a poem ("Orgy," also in S.P., p. 89) comparing artists to bees devoured by ants for the sake of the sweetness they have gathered. There is a nice contrast here with the last poem in the same collection, "No Choice," with its dry complaint about the inadequacy of metaphor.

In all of these cases the poet appears in the third person. It would be rash to take any of these statements out of their contexts and use them as elements of a credo, but it is interesting to note that when the narrator/poet appears in the first person the images are more ambivalent, the tenor more sombre, as in "Saturday Morning" (M., p. 31)—

> And here I sit,
> Flameswallower who gulps down flame and then
> Puffs out stale air that turns to flame again.

Or in "A Good Day" (R.A., p. 56):

> A heron, folded round himself,
> Stands in the ebb, as I in mine.
> I feel my world beneath me, like his, shelving
> To darker depths of dark and bitter brine.

While in "Dispossessed" (R.L., p. 60) a number of characteristic themes are hinted at, the middle stanza goes:

> Ishmael among the phenomena, I hide
> In unreal deserts. Boredom is my weather
> And bitterness the water in its wells.
> Grave facts go by and pitch their tents together;
> Their night-fire tells
> Me to observe that light and keep outside
> In my own darkness where no moon can be,
> Since I've destroyed it for not being me.

And the poem ends:

> While I (what I?) prowl through the dark and stare
> At a night-fire and myself sitting there.

The poet as his own doppelganger, as his own Dr Foster, arguing with himself . . .

Notes

R.L.—*Riding Lights* (The Hogarth Press, 1955).

S.S.—*The Sinai Sort* (*ditto*, 1957).

C.G.—*A Common Grace* (Chatto and Windus with The Hogarth Press, 1960).

R.A.—*A Round of Applause* (*ditto*, 1962).

M.—*Measures* (*ditto*, 1965).

S.—*Surroundings* (*ditto*, 1966).

R.T.—*Rings on a Tree* (*ditto*, 1968).

M.P.—*A Man in My Position* (*ditto*, 1969).

S.P.—*Selected Poems* (The Hogarth Press, 1971).

W.B.—*The White Bird* (Chatto and Windus with The Hogarth Press, 1973).

(For ease of reference, when a poem is available both in an earlier collection and in the selected volume, page references for both are given.)

1. There is an interesting comparison with the development of W. S. Graham's poetry. Graham's earlier work—*The Seven Journeys* (McLellan, Glasgow, (1944), *2nd Poems* (Nicholson and Watson, London, 1945) and *The White Threshold* (Faber, 1949)—belongs to an area very similar to that of MacCaig's

work of the forties. *The Night Fishing* (Faber, 1955) appeared in the same year as MacCaig's *Riding Lights*, yet the break with the earlier modes is much less clean. It was another fifteen years (during which MacCaig brought out another seven collections) before Graham's next book appeared, *Malcolm Mooney's Land* (Faber, 1970). Here too, there are still traces of poetic habits developed in the forties. At its strongest, as in the title poems of the 1955 and 1970 collections, Graham's work can be felt to succeed against the odds of a not very fruitful legacy; at its weakest, his work seems to be stifled by the legacy, by worry about the very possibility of communication.

2. See "Explicit Snow" (*C.G.*, p. 9), 11. 13–15; "Not Stolen, but Strayed" (*S.*, p. 39), 11. 14–17.

3. See "Absorbed" (*S.*, p. 57).

4. See also "All Being Equal," "Poachers, Early Morning," "Mutual Life," "Loch na Berraig" and "Brackloch" in *R.A.*, pp 21, 38, 42, 48 and 50. None of these are in *S.P.*

5. See pp 39, 41, 50, 54, 56.

6. See pp 9, 13, 19, 21, 22, 39, 40, 45, 53–54, 57, 59, 60. Again, none of these are in *S.P.*

7. See also *C.G.*, pp 11, 38; *R.A.*, p. 14; *M.*, p. 29.

8. See *R.L.*, p. 46; *S.S.*, p. 41; *C.G.*, p. 31 (*S.P.*, p. 38); *R.A.*, pp 15 (*S.P.*, p. 55), 42, 50, 54, 58, 61; *M.*, p. 32 (*S.P.*, p. 73); *S.*, pp 33, 53, 57; *M.P.*, pp 30, 59 (*S.P.*, p. 118).

9. See "No End, No Beginning," *M.P.*, p. 26 and *S.P.*, p. 113; "Centre of Centres," *Scotsman*, 1:5:71; and "Inward Bound," *W.B.*, p. 35.

10. See "Progress," "Smuggler," "Responsibility," "Leader of Men" in *S.*, pp 13, 21, 22, 29; "Balances" in *R.T.*, p. 10; "Types," "The Unlikely," "Power Dive," "Academic" in *M.P.*, pp 34, 58, 60, 61. None of these are in *S.P.*

11. "You Went Away," "Double Life," "Drifter," "Country House," "Empty Pool," "False Summer" in *R.L.*, pp 18, 30, 42, 47, 50, 54. These were all retained in *S.P.*—pp 12, 15, 21, 17, 22, 23.

12. Both MacCaig and Crichton Smith are featured in Penguin Modern Poets 21: Morgan perhaps would have made a more suitable third member than George Mackay Brown. Morgan was included earlier in this series (No. 15) in the improbable company of Alan Bold and Edward Brathwaite.

CONTEXTS

IV

GEOGRAPHICAL AND SOCIAL

IF WE THINK OF POETS whose work is rooted in a defined locality, Norman Nicholson is bound to come to mind. For the sense of belonging which his poetry celebrates is at one with his way of life: having spent all his time in Millom, what he writes about are the things and the people which have surrounded him for decades, and however densely woven his verse may become, it never forgets for long that talking familiarity which suggests a settled and easy ambience. It would be rash to conclude that while Nicholson begins local he also remains local.[1] On the contrary, Robin Skelton has written this: "What is most concrete, most factual, and most particular in his environment is always also most revelatory of the larger spiritual dimensions. What is most limited by the awareness of life's brevity is most indicative of the vaster perspective of pre-history, and the evolutionary process . . . The "regionalism" of Norman Nicholson is his mode of establishing the human need of the familiar, in order that he may place it in the perspective of unknown and disturbing considerations. He creates, speck by speck, and brilliantly, a landscape as vivid, concrete, and well documented as that of Hardy's Wessex, and one much more detailed and less misty than that of his revered Wordsworth."[2] It is doubtful if Wordsworth was interested in quite that kind of detail, but Skelton's general point is an important one.

If we turn to a poet like Seamus Heaney we find a less absolute mode of belonging to a locality, for there is clearly some disjunction between Heaney's continuing autobiographical reality and the lush, water-logged, laborious cycle of small-farm life which is the raw material of so much of his poetry. We cannot dismiss this simply by pointing out that in Ireland (as, for instance, in Scandinavia) the realities of country life are closer to a larger proportion of the people than is the case in long-industrialised areas of England. Yet it would be unjust to see in Heaney's devotion to bawn and mossland a mere avoidance of current realities: these can break through very sharply, even when the context seems remote, as in the closing lines of "The Tollund Man" in *Wintering Out*:

> Out there in Jutland
> In the old man-killing parishes
> I will feel lost,
> Unhappy and at home.

93

Questions of locality frequently arise in reviews of Scottish poetry, if for no other reason than that metropolitan reviewers sometimes assume that "local" is synonymous with "remote." There is no Scottish poet with the absolute kind of local loyalty we find in Nicholson—unless we refer to George Mackay Brown, though in that context there are important differences. Again, there are none with quite the devotion to rustic life evident in Heaney. But in many Scottish poets we do find highly developed forms of the ambiguities briefly suggested in connection with Heaney's treatment of his locale.

Edwin Morgan, for instance, "belongs" to Glasgow, but in a metropolis there are innumerable overlapping modes of belonging which may yet be very far apart from each other. Thus while he may describe, with percipience and sympathy, the "stalled lives" and their surroundings, he does so as an observer from a very different kind of life. Moreover, one of the principal themes of his poetry is the tension between a local loyalty and a hunger for distant exotic places: the local environment may be seen with clear knowledge of both its grime and its promise, yet there is always a need for imaginings about places like Timor or Saturn or the future.

> We take in
> the dream, a cloth from the line
> the trains fling sparks on
> in our city. We're better awake.
> But you know I'd take
> you all the same,
> if you were my next stranger.
>
> ("Floating off to Timor")

Iain Crichton Smith's local roots are of course strong, both personally and in his poetry, and this sense of locality is accentuated by the particular beleaguered situation of his Gaelic background. Again, there is nothing blind about this loyalty:

> To have fallen in love with
> stone, thistle and strath,
> to see the blood flow
> in wandering old rivers,

94

this wound is not staunched
by handkerchiefs or verse.
This wound was after all
love and a deep curse.

At the same time, the voracious nature of his imagination is liable
to absorb imagery from any locality whatever, either for the sake
of an analogy to a condition nearer home—

Ah, you Russians, how often I feel like you . . .
. . .
For something is happening everywhere but here.
Here there are Hamlets and old generals.
Everyone sighs and says "ekh" and in the stream
a girl is swimming naked among gnats.
This space is far too much for us like time.
Even the clocks have asthma . . .

—or for the sake of discerning a common condition in spite of an
apparent contrast, as in "For Ann in America in the Autumn:"

O hills of the Far Country you're so blue
and dead and quiet. The old clouds drift through
the old mind. The weighted earth prevails.
We're hauled towards gravity by the worn heels.

In such cases the focus on the distant locality need not be clear:
the raw elements caught up into the imagery may indeed, like the
literary reminiscences in "How often I feel like you" or "Russian
Poem," be rather banal. [3]

With the exception of a few poems set in America and Italy,
the bulk of Norman MacCaig's work draws its imagery from
Edinburgh (where he lives) and West Sutherland (where he spends
summers). At an elementary level his poems begin from what he
sees, first hand, but there, in the very process of seeing, is where
the ambiguities begin. His poems return again and again to their
familiar localities (look at the place-names on a map of Assynt,
for instance) but they are not necessarily experienced, in the poems,
as home anchor-points. In the mind observing them they are indeed
highly unstable and subject to the most improbable transformations.
A poem like "High up on Suilven" [4] celebrates not a sense of belonging to a familiar place but the similes and metaphors which it
startles in the poet's mind.

> A web like this
> Has a thread that goes beyond the possible

—and the home-ground of much of MacCaig's poetry is not in the primary scene but in this interplay between actuality and possibility: the local geographical detail may well turn out to be incidental. In "Lesson,"[5] for instance, he looks at a fish-box, or at least tries to look at it:

> He tries to see just what it is.
> He counts the slats it's made of—
> sides, top and bottom—
> and reads, in neat red letters,
> RETURN TO LOCHINVER. He notices
> sixpences of scales, gone grubby.
> And then he's stuck.
> He goes off knowing
> he hasn't seen the fishbox at all.

But the objects observed seldom remain passive for in the process of observation they are liable to become any number of other things, either playfully or menacingly. So when we look at Edinburgh or Lochinver through MacCaig's poems, the images spilling round the distorting lens are so agile that we cannot be sure we are seeing these places at all.

> Meantime the fishbox
> waits till it's night. Then
> like a pterodactyl it planes
> through the darkness and flies into
> the sleeper's mind. It opens
> and crams the sleeper inside it.
> And when the hammer hits
> the first nail on the head,
> he wakes with a scream, he knows
> what a fishbox is, he knows
> what a rope is, or a seagull standing
> at its horrible attention.

* * *

There are three other poets whose work can be discussed more fully in this context: George Bruce, Derick Thomson and George Mackay Brown. Despite very different responses to their home territories, respectively the north-east, Lewis and Orkney, they can be grouped together here for purposes of discussion because their poetic dependence on their local roots is of a more direct kind than any we find in Morgan, Crichton Smith or MacCaig. And this dependence, while more directly strong, is at the same time a measure of certain limitations.

George Bruce's *Collected Poems*[6] begins and ends with poems about poems. The first of these describes his poems as songs although their dominant pace and tone are those of a deliberative talking voice; it also refers to the desire to achieve a "taut" music. The last poem in the book is called "Making a Poem"—

> Some days words come at the run
> like boys for supper.
> Clean and firm
> they present themselves
> alert and at attention.
> These days are worth waiting for.

We notice the qualities of directness implied by "clean and firm," "alert and at attention," though the boarding-school simile is a little surprising in its suggestion of limitations being accepted in the possibilities of language. Women may be fickle, alluring, ambiguous in ways which many poets have likened to language itself: eager, nicely-washed schoolboys can be expected to behave when they are told to.

The constant features of Bruce's verse—the limited number of elemental images, the stressed moral concern, the careful articulation —can readily be associated with the landscapes and social habits of his native region. Iain Crichton Smith has described Bruce's verse as an exact notation for the north-east. "It is, as he himself says, a 'land without myth' and he is never tempted to import into it alien opulences of language. It is a land of hard light . . . It is a land where towns seem slightly irrelevant against ageless rocks and sea: it is an almost anti-poetic land that requires a terse language, abrupt, physical. It is an astringent land."[7] But it must be added that Bruce is as much concerned with interpretation as with notation and that his language is frequently abstract as well as physical. An extreme comment on this predilection for the abstract has been made by David Craig, with reference to "Kinnaird Head," a poem which begins:

> I go North to cold, to home, to Kinnaird,
> Fit monument for our time . . .

and ends:

> The water plugs in the cliff sides,
> The gull cries from the clouds
> This is the consummation of the plain.
>
> O impregnable and very ancient rock,
> Rejecting the violence of water,
> Ignoring its accumulations and strategy,
> You yield to history nothing.

Craig comments: "This is laughably solemn. Each word, whenever the poem goes beyond the simplest Imagist image, has such an air of saying so much, like an old owl that fancies itself wise. But the abstractions — 'consummation,' 'rejecting,' 'strategy' — are there only because T. S. Eliot had meditated on history in 'Gerontion.' This way with the stark and simple—contrasted with George Campbell Hay's or Sorley Maclean's— seems to me traditional in a wholly weak sense. 'Home' is supposed to stand for a timeless, basic *pietas*; but it remains just a word."[8]

If we can ignore the critical over-kill here, we can see that Craig touches upon a potential and at times actual weakness in the basic fabric of Bruce's verse: the anxiety to *explain*. A line like this

> The beach jarred by white stones

with its effective use of "jarred" is not characteristic because more commonly the physical objects in his verse, as well as his descriptions of them, are unambiguous, spare and as if deliberately unexciting, in case too close a physical response may distract from the controlling meaning. In a poem for Henry Moore he states an artistic ideal which entails a process of definition and encompassing and a devotion to present, particular experience, yet in the ensuing list

of images (e.g. "the tree in the garden") what we have is the archetypal, not the eccentric. In another poem he refers to Shetland as a
land "that tells the cosmic tale/of earth and sky and water." And
in "Reflection at Sixty" he recalls a "wax moustachioed purple
uncle" who advised him to give up "all this bother about meaning."[9]
Now this concern to define and encompass, to listen to the cosmic
tale, to persist with the bother about meaning, can be over-riding:
the search for the Word can do great damage to the words. At its
most positive and achieved, his verse does communicate a moral
firmness at one with the landscapes and characters it describes.
At the same time, the borderline between hardness and softness
can be devious and indistinct.

As for the geographical context itself, we are seldom allowed to
see the land without being reminded of the human labour it demands:

> Years back the stones were lifted from the fields,
> The animals driven to their holes, the land drained,
> Dug, planted, the ground pieced out.
> The heather was beat. The crop grew
> On the hill. The paths were trod.
> The land was peopled and tilled.
> This is the land without myth.[10]

This last line—which occurs six times in the poem—offers a naked
assertion after the careful factual description of the taming of the
land. Yet that very description, reduced to elementary essentials,
implies the archetypal nature of those processes, as if the groundwork
for myth were being turned over.

> Accept the sublit seas beneath—the squid,
> The pink and purple prostrates, valvular jellies,
> Fungoid jungle. Here globe, tube, cone, the final shapes
> Have life, have mouths, erupt, move in currents
> Without air and are still—lives crepuscular.
> With these lands I have no acquaintance.[11]

There is an even greater distancing of the physical here. First we
have an injunction ("accept") which draws attention to the undersea
world not simply as an object of contemplation but as a subject
towards which we must adopt an attitude; then we have the latinate,

99

literary words ("sublit," "crepuscular") and the diagrammatic descriptions of the life-forms ("globe," "tube," "cone"). This is however not inappropriate for a man whose feet are firmly on dry land, who admits he has no acquaintance with the sea-floor. He seems to be cannily restraining his imagination from venturing into areas which have not been tested and surveyed in daylight.

What gives the north-east its character is the conflict between land and sea, or more exactly the tenacious defence of the former against the latter.

> The kirk looks graceless, a block house
> To defy the last snort of winter,
> The house shouldering the sea,
> Dark as your ship inside, the windows locked,
> The curtains heavy as if suspecting light.
> . . .
> Blind backs to the blind sea;
> Something was being said by them
> In their silence, while the wind blurted about
> Their stone corners that stood on stone,
> And the muffled talk of waters
> Fell from those shut windows.

The personifications ("defy," "shouldering," "suspecting," "blind backs") suggest a moral as well as a physical toughness in face of the harsh conditions that threaten survival. And the words denoting violent action ("snort," "blurted") stop short of any high onomato-poeic quality or verbal excitement, as if in these stern circumstances mere word-play were a frivolity. Yet there is a soft spot, for what are we to make of "something?"[12]

Bruce's handling of this type of sea-imagery and of the implications he draws out, can be contrasted with, say, the concentration on the physical that we find in Norman Nicholson. In the opening verse of "The Black Guillemot" (in *A Local Habitation*) both metaphor ("adrift," "flowering") and simile ("red as dogwood") operate in conjunction with precise geographical location to guide our attention closely onto the scene observed. Later in the poem we learn that the poet is looking through binoculars, a significant indication of the poem's concentration on *seeing*.

Midway between Fleswick and St Bees North Head,
The sun in the west,
All Galloway adrift on the horizon;
The sandstone red
As dogwood; sea-pink, sea-campion and the sea itself
Flowering in clefts of the cliff—
And down on one shelf,
Dozen on dozen pressed side by side together,
White breast by breast,
Beaks to the rock and tails to the fish-stocked sea,
The guillemots rest.

Or we may consider another contrast, this time with the fluidity and bravado with which Iain Crichton Smith will pursue concrete image and resonant abstraction simultaneously: mind and eye respond as one and we do not stop to ask whether he is observing *or* interpreting.

Against your will I set the changing tones
of water swarming over lucid stones
and salmon bubbling in repeated suns.

Against your death I let the tide come in
with its weight of water and its lack of sin,
the opulent millions of a rising moon.

(Elegy 16 of *Love Poems and Elegies*)

Bruce's landscapes are populated of course and it is here, in personal and family history and in observation of local character and ways of life that we find the kind of individual detail whose recording helps to counteract the abstracting tendency associated with descriptions of elementary and archetypal natural processes. The second piece in *Collected Poems*, "Inheritance," affirms a sense of belonging to a family, which in turn is rooted in the activities of the area: "Not I write,/But, perhaps William Bruce,/Cooper." And the recording of childhood memories may, by focussing sharply on a few details, suggest implications which are elsewhere dissipated by being too earnestly spelt out. Such implications may reach further than home concerns, as in "Visitations from a War-time Childhood" with its blend of childhood reminiscence and adult comment. [13]

101

Descriptions of local character, such as in "Praising Aberdeen-shire Farmers"—

> This is the East coast with winter
> Written into its constitution
> And so is very productive of men
> Who do not wait for good
> In case there is none.

—such descriptions have an authority of local provenance which is absent from the intently observed yet archetypal scenes from Italy, like that of the mother and child on the train leaving Florence, with her paradoxical distance from and closeness to the figures preserved in paintings from another age. We can sense the local provenance even more sharply in sketches of individual characters, such as "Cheery Sam," where the character's own words ("These were his words") attest the documentary truth of the portrait and the poet's own words (Sam's boots are "deep in squeaking herring") add a further elucidation.[14]

In general Bruce's language operates on quite a different level from the language actually used in the region. His tone may be that of a man deliberating and talking, but the language is decidedly that of a lettered man, accommodating abstractions, literary reminiscences, biblical quotations, and, in its weaker moments, echoing the Eliot of the *Four Quartets* or Edwin Muir at his more generalised. Bruce *can* record local speech, but it is interesting to see that when he does he lays before us the very contrast between this speech and the linguistic fabric of his own poetic mode.

> *Andra and Jockie*
> *Scutter wi the tractor*
> *Jean's i the kitchie*
> *Dod's i the byre*
> *Fred the orra loon*
> *Chops kindlin for the fire.*

> Late springs this North, hard the sun,
> Caller the wind that blows to the bone.[15]

Despite "caller" (fresh), the English here is doubly distanced from the Scots: first in being English, second in being non-colloquial

102

English. The poet's forebears may well have belonged socially and linguistically to the world invoked by the lines in Scots, but the poet himself does not, as his juxtaposition of the two sensibilities shows. In "The Singers"[16] we see another example of this kind of juxtaposition. The bulk of the poem is a celebration of the sea- and landscapes of the north-east and their traditional occupations. As a series of anchor-points and as a kind of documentation, the English is interrupted four times by a pair of stanzas in Scots recounting the voyage of a fishing boat, a voyage entailing danger, a good catch and a fatal accident. The poet's commentary on the local way of life develops the idea stated elsewhere that this is a land without myth; "our sea . . . was not unsimilar to Homer's ocean," yet

> Where, where are the singers,
> Where the winged instruments of celebration?

If we think of the potency of ancient myth that is still available to modern Greek poets we have a measure of the fact that for Scotland, even in the Celtic west, there is no equivalent availability. Yet, again as we saw before, the raw material of the lives described is the raw material out of which such myths grew: the concrete details serve archetypal generalisations.

Finally, we could refer to three poems which gather together Bruce's most characteristic preoccupations.[17] In all three, his habitual view of the elemental struggle between sea and land, between nature and man, is focussed by local history; and in all three the use of language has a crucial bearing on the handling of the material.

In "A Gateway to the Sea (I)," subtitled "At the East Port, St Andrews," the language of both the opening and the close fails to engage directly with the intention of the poem, the first through overstatement and the second through understatement, but in the main bulk of the poem the language does engage fully in a way that allows a meditative circling in time, with a central focus on simple human values. A preference is declared for "this handled stone, now ruined," for among the usual debris of history, such as "rings, diamants, snuff boxes, warships," we find

> Also the less worthy garments of worthy men.

In "The Island" the historical context is advantageously narrowed to family history: the poem is about Bruce's grandfather, who was one of the earliest herring-curers to set up a fishing station in Balta-sound. The Scots used in the course of the poem is a more integral part of the total fabric than in the instances mentioned above: it is not marked off by italics, though occasional words or phrases are either quoted as speech or signalled by inverted commas. It remains strictly incidental to the main vehicle of English, and in the one stanza where it is used "straight" it acts as a means of social differentiation. Thirdly, in "Moon Men," a sequence of eight short poems, the references to the moon-landings in parts I, V and VIII give a startling new context for the age-old patterns of the fishermen's lives. The astronauts come back from the moon—and Jeems Buchan comes back from "the moon controlled Yarmouth fishing." The contrast is certainly not to the disadvantage of the Buchan family: indeed the sceptical view of the astronauts is quite in keeping with the canny appraisal which a north-east fisherman may give to an alleged big-shot or hero. For all their "marvels of precision" in distant parts what the astronauts return to is "the unknowable earth." And their efforts to perform a solemn ritual on the moon— trying to arrest their rolling and bouncing long enough to plant the Stars and Stripes to canned music—are in farcical contrast to the rooted, familiar ritual of work and season which is the lifelong experience of the fishermen. The poem is entirely in English but part VII raises the language question explicitly in a form which we can relate to Bruce's own use of language, and in a form which clearly bears wide social implications. Jeems Buchan meets Joseph MacLeod (the "famous war-time announcer") and each expresses an admiration for the speech of the other.

> These were not civilities.
> Both had spoken truth
> to their disadvantage.

* * *

The traumatic events of Edwin Muir's early experience—his transition from a pre-industrial childhood on an Orkney farm to a harsh and tragic adolescence in Glasgow—led him by sheer force of personal experience to contemplate such age-old antitheses as Innocence and Experience, Eden and Fall. However critical opinion may waver about the effectiveness with which he relived the ancient myths in terms of his poetry, it is worth stressing the fact of this personal experience: his predilection for myth was not simply a matter of seeking out literary devices but had an important therapeutic aspect. Bruce's poetry does not entail this element of personal stress, but he does seem to share (as in a more extreme form does George Mackay Brown) something of Muir's sensibility in that his view of the perennial landscapes and activities of his native region is controlled by a desire to delineate archetypal patterns.

When we turn to the poetry of Derick Thomson[18] we find both a more richly detailed personal history and a sharper focus on social, economic and linguistic circumstances. The fact that Thomson passed his childhood and boyhood on the island of Lewis and perforce has spent his adult life in very different surroundings gives a very distinct temporal and spatial context to his memories of earlier life: these make up the stock of images through which he explores his own entrapment in time. Yet those very years, the twenties and early thirties, coincided with the last years of a fully indigenous communal life in the area, so that his memories of boyhood are inextricably linked with his feelings about the erosion of Gaelic society. A degree of nostalgia is inevitable but, as we shall see, the sense of regret in Thomson's poetry is often qualified by other elements. Moreover, his role as a Gaelic writer is not confined to his poetry for while in that poetry he may explore the ambiguities and shifting connections between the past and the present, as they affect both himself as an individual and the society to which he belongs, he is also actively engaged as a scholar, entrepreneur and propagandist in a wide range of very practical activities aimed at preserving and reviving the culture of that society.[19]

In a broadcast talk Thomson has touched upon both these shaping influences from his early years—the close physical experience of a particular landscape and the contact with a traditional Gaelic world. "Bayble was then a village of about one thousand inhabitants, Garrabost about half that size. They were coastal villages, as practically all Lewis villages are, one on each side of the Point peninsula. Down the centre lay a long band of quite deserted moorland, where you could walk for miles out of sight of houses. The same conditions apply in many other parts of the island with much larger distances involved, and if Lewis has a private spirit

105

or genius (as distinct from its evident communal one) it resides in these moors. I fell in love with them early . . . Bayble in the late twenties and in the early thirties was still securely in the Gaelic world. The dialogue with the outside world had begun of course, but it was cautious and halting and intermittent. There were still a fair number of people who spoke little or no English, and many who spoke a rich, colourful self-sufficient Gaelic . . . I knew a good few people who had virtually escaped the net of compulsory schooling, even if they had put in a few months in the new schools, and I am glad to have had that link with my unspoilt, unadulterated Gaelic forebears, who were the heirs of so many centuries of Gaelic history . . . The relationship with Lewis has occupied my thoughts as a poet at many times, and finally it seemed necessary to look long and hard at this preoccupation, to lift it up and examine it from many angles. That is too cold and static an image: the process was scarcely as deliberate as that. At any rate, the sequence of poems called *An Rathad Cian* or *The Far Road* came into being in this way, written in Glasgow . . . "[20] *The Far Road* is a varied sequence of 56 short poems. That the Gaelic poet should translate his own work from the minority into the majority language, and that many of his readers even within Scotland have to depend on this process, is symptomatic of his embattled position. Nonetheless, even when discussion is limited to a translated version, the main features of his preoccupations are clearly visible.

It need hardly be said that Lewis is the geographical anchor, but it is perhaps worth stressing that the place-names are not just reference points on a map: they are the names of living communities and, moreover, with their frequent mixture of Norse and Celtic elements, they indicate a deep historical context. Occasionally too a startling spatial context is suggested:

> At daybreak you set out
> for Swordale moor.
> It was hardly reminiscent of the pampas,
> but you had your dog at heel
> and spoke to him in Spanish. (No. 17)

But the Lewis in Thomson's poetry has a parallel, non-geographical existence in the poet's mind and feelings. It has been subjected to the alchemy of memory and appears in many different transformations: it is a monster (No. 1), a sweetheart (Nos. 4 and 9), an ancient pillar-stone (No. 12), a loom "in a locked outhouse" (No. 14), and as a boat which sets out hopefully to the fishing:

> You thought the herring were thick
> in your path, woven on the green,
> nap on warp and weft,
> but you were wrong.
> When you looked again
> there was nothing but herringbone
> and your hand cold in paralysis.
> When I looked at you again
> I saw your name written in large letters
> METAGAMA.

(The *Metagama* was an emigrant ship which left Lewis in the early twenties; and of course "herringbone" carries an allusion also to weaving.)

The nostalgia, too, is on several levels. It is relatively straightforward in references to "that world in shards about my feet" (No. 4), to "a coffinful of songs" being laid in the earth (No. 52), and to separation as a disease akin to weightlessness:

> I escaped the pull of your planet,
> my step is weightless, heavy though middle age may be,
> on these well-known roads,
> I float alone in space.

It is not however simply a matter of regretting a lost security: while No. 7 recalls the feel of bare feet on the moor in childhood, nostalgically, in No. 8 the moor is also treacherous and even predatory:

> The heaving, billowy fruitful bog
> lying there till eternity
> with its mouth open,
> swallowing sheep,
> and men,
> and me.

When socially orientated the nostalgia sharpens into bitter complaint, a process we can observe in "Coffins," from his 1967 collection.[21]

107

The first half records memories of his grandfather, a joiner; the second half then uses this imagery in a manner common to propaganda, though it is worth noting how the bitterness is directed as much towards indifference within the beleaguered society as towards intrusion from without. To return to *The Far Road*, we can find acrid comments on the usual attempts to revitalise island life:

> Donald Cam, my boy,
> if you were to keep to the Uig hills now
> you would have more to show for it than you had:
> a house from the Board, and a subsidy from the Crofters
>   Commission. (No. 31)

More to *show*, because it is easy to modernise old houses and crofts through government charity, but quite another matter to revitalise a way of life. In the village at death's door "the cradle will rot in the new barn with its zinc roof" (No. 19). What is absent is the particular quality of life which Thomson not only knows *about* as a scholar but recalls as memories of certain remarkable individuals he knew when young, and it is this contact which is

> . . . the key to my museum,
> the record on which I play my folklore,
> the trowel with which I turn the ground
> of the age that is now gone,
> the image that keeps control over false images.

At the level where the poet recognises the apparent insolubility of his dilemma yet refuses to abandon it, the nostalgia is clearly only one element in a complex response:

> The heart tied to a tethering post, round upon round of rope
> till it grows short,
> and the mind free.
> I bought its freedom dearly.

No. 53 does in fact propose a return and coldly accepts its cruel unreality: yet the evidence of the secret cave, as distinct from the open street, means that such acceptance is surely not absolute. There would, in truth, be no "return"—

I remembered Lot's wife,
and yet, and yet,
I am going to be a memorial-pillar.

Fed by memory
which makes me grow
in this dark cave,
awaiting the turn of the tide,
and crouching under my load
in this green cave without noon.

*   *   *

The coalescence in Thomson's poetry of obsessive personal longing and a sense of agonised involvement with a particular type of society is remarkable; few other British poets are in a position to respond in quite this manner to such a predicament. In George Mackay Brown's poetry there is an even stronger aspect to the poet's communal role, but it rests on a basis which could hardly be more different. Mackay Brown has spent his life in Orkney and has no wish to live anywhere else, yet despite the fact that his family and personal history is intimately rooted in the locality that history has no part in his poetry. His poetic role, in many respects anachronistic, is that of the impersonal craftsman who records and celebrates the life of the community. Moreover, while the apparent models of this role (such as the Norse bards) were much concerned with the events and personalities of their own day, Mackay Brown's concern with contemporary society is tangential and uncomfortable. The communal life he celebrates is one that has all but vanished: it can be seen only now and then in ghostly outlines behind the actual mid-twentieth century life of Orkney. The function of "recording" is not therefore as simple as it may seem: it also entails a strong element of selection and interpretation.

Given the role that Mackay Brown has assumed, then, many of the other functions of poetry are automatically excluded. Agonies, joys, ambiguities there may well be—but not as the individual poet has experienced them, only in so far as they are the common property of the community. It follows too that accessibility is an important factor. Thus the limitations of Mackay Brown's work appear to have been consciously accepted.

We can observe them at three levels. At the formal level, his

109

reliance on formulae is striking. For not only do catalogues and lists prevail, but the length of such forms is more often than not determined by the magic numbers 3 and 7, especially the latter. Thus we have poems listing 7 characters, perhaps crewmen ("Shipwreck"), brothers ("The Abbot"), farmers at market ("Hamnavoe Market"). In "Country Girl" we have 7 womanly functions, in "Weather Bestiary" 7 types of weather, in "The Hawk" 7 days of the week corresponding to 7 acts of the hawk, in "The Condemned Well" 7 visitors to the well, and in "The Seven Houses" 7 doors leading to 7 houses corresponding to 7 stages in human life.[22] An occasional variation gives us a list of 3 ("Viking Testament"—ox, dove, rose) or 5 ("The Five Voyages of Arnor").[23] Even the details in many poems occur in 3's, or 7's—3 wounds, 3 arches, 3 women at the tree, 3 birds, 3 Fridays, 3 ploughs, 3 sets of questions, 3 princes; 7 sounds of the sea, 7 curses, 7 oceans, 7 stars, 7 scythes, 7 agricultural shows . . . One soon feels it would be very upsetting to come across an Orkney field with more than 7 cows, or a man awkwardly blessed with 10 fingers.

In his diction Mackay Brown shows a similar predilection for formulae, particularly of the kind associated with riddles and kennings: the purple samurae of the flood (lobsters), poor tooth-relish (dog-fish), gold beast (sun), gold whale (sun), floating feast-halls (whales), a lady of butter (cow), petrol-drinker (tractor). It is a short step from here to types of over-writing which, in their arch cultivation of literary echoes, consort ill with the role Mackay Brown clearly adopts in general. In one type we have tenuous blends of traditional imagery:

> The shaken branch, The Voice, the draped
> Whispering coil of flame,
> And Eve a tall unfingered harp
> Strung with desire and shame.

In another we have grotesque and over-reaching metaphor:

> Sunset drives a butcher blade
> In the day's throat.

In others, particularly in the treacherous boglands of the "prose-poem," we have deliberate pastiche which appears to be taken too seriously to be considered as parody:

. . . and there I would have stopped to warm me a while (these tribes exist pure, birth to death, in a fire of simple pagan lust), but that a far behest lured me towards a consummation so beautiful that we but echo the ecstasy with harps and statues; as the naked tinker boy held now to the shell of his ear a colder sea mouth.[24]

In contrast we could point to, say, the closing lines of "Thorfinn":[25]

> A crofter at early light
> Found an empty boat stuttering on the rocks
> And dawn-cold cocks cheering along the links.

Both "stuttering" and "cheering" are sharp at the literal descriptive level, and moreover contribute effectively to the context: the meaningless stuttering contrasts with the silence of death and the cheerless cheering coldly asserts the indifferent continuance of natural life. We could point also to a more characteristic example of his cleaner, chiselled language in the short poem "Taxman:" its scale may be miniature but its ordering of the few details establishes a communal situation with its inherent drama yet leaves no room for obtrusive literary echoes or historical question-begging.

> Seven scythes leaned at the wall.
> Beard upon golden beard
> The last barley load
> Swayed through the yard.
> The girls uncorked the ale.
> Fiddle and feet moved together.
> Then between stubble and heather
> A horseman rode.[26]

There is, too, an interesting feature in "The Drowning Brothers." As they drown, transforming from flesh to marble, images of the hillside burn flicker through their minds.

> The burn is a fish in a net of fences . . .
> The burn is a glancing shuttle . . .

But while in almost any other poem by Mackay Brown these images would be allowed to accumulate for their own sake, here they are distanced and dramatised into a precise context which has an absolute conclusion:

111

Heavy with images, the statues drowned.[27]

Nevertheless the reservations I have indicated do have serious consequences. The elemental images of birth, marriage, death, of wave and field, fish and corn, fiddle and ale, tend to be moved round like counters in all too predictable patterns. Through phrases like "crucifixion of the seed" or lines like "The ploughman turns/ Furrow by holy furrow/The liturgy of April . . . " religious significance is asserted merely by juxtaposing ecclesiastical and natural imagery. In turn this leads to an over-all lack of presentness, and despite the oft-remarked frailty of human life, a lack of disturbance. The drowned fishermen and their black widows are like formalised figures in a tapestry. Look at Mackay Brown's hawk on the fourth day of his week:

> And on Wednesday he fell on a bush
> And the blackbird
> Laid by his little flute for the last time.

and on the sixth:

> And on Saturday he fell on Bigging
> And Jock lowered his gun
> And nailed a small wing over the corn.[28]

Despite the effectiveness of "small" the hawk is contained in his cycle and need not unduly trouble us. But look at Ted Hughes' hawk, in *Lupercal*:

> No arguments assert my right:
>
> The sun is behind me.
> Nothing has changed since I began.
> My eye has permitted no change.
> I am going to keep things like this.

Neither is "real," in the sense that both are created by rhetoric, but we cannot avoid being affected by the implications of the latter. We can register this difference while at the same time recognising that Mackay Brown is not interested in effects like Hughes' and achieves his own effects deliberately.

The kind of achievement he aims at is clearly related to his view of Orkney's past and present. In Thomson's case the view of personal and communal past, and of the actual losses and possibilities within a particular society, are very clearly realised. But Mackay Brown's attitude to Orkney's past is ambivalent and subject to romantic over-simplifications. Not many of his historical sketches have the sober concentration on the subject that we find in a piece like "Buonaparte, the Laird, and the Volunteers."[29] He is liable to make references back in time in order to gain a stance from which he can militate against the kind of society most of us in North Europe and North America now live. In *An Orkney Tapestry* (1969) he is quite explicit about this. One wonders how closely in touch he is with the way of life he professes to reject: for example he rails against "Progress" as the "new religion" as if he had just discovered it and in terms mildly reminiscent of Chesterton but in fact who does now have any such illusions? His particular interest in material progress is of course related to its effect in the local social history of his area, and that is a different matter—"the notion of progress is a cancer that makes an elemental community look better, and induces a false euphoria, while it drains the life out of it remorselessly." But how many questions does "elemental" beg? There are even more specious references to "the atom-and-planet horror at the heart of our civilisation," and so on. Over against the alleged false gods of the new age he sets qualities derived from religious tradition both pagan and christian, but again such a reference is utilised to show that all the rest of us are out of step: "The ancient magical ceremonial quality of art makes it profoundly suspect to all puritans, hedonists, humanists, democrats, pragmatists, rationalists, progressives; and nowadays nearly everyone fits into one or other of these categories." There is little in all this on which we can take a firm grip—which is hardly surprising when the author himself admits that he is interested in facts only "as they tend and gesture, like birds and grass and waves, in 'the gale of life'." But facts are chiels etc, and the gale of life has a habit of blowing not where it listeth but where the prophet wants it to blow.[30]

This aspect of Mackay Brown's attitude cannot be ignored but it is worth stressing that it is most evident when his work is at its weakest. This applies particularly to his fiction—and here some brief comment should be made on his fiction because, in contrast to Iain Crichton Smith, the poetry can be seen as incidental to the best of his stories. Granted, when the fiction is at its least effective it can be discussed entirely on the level of the assumptions I have indicated. His pseudo-historical reconstructions are least credible when they are manipulated to show that the new life is shabbier than the old one.[31] His historical fiction succeeds when his focus is not on the alleged primal virtues of the unsophisticated peasantry but on the human predicament of, say, an individual tragedy as in "Witch." The contrast between the old civilisation and the new is seldom handled satisfactorily because of an *a priori* reluctance to see the new without revulsion, though there is one story ("The Wireless Set") which makes a most pointed use of this contrast. A fisherman reacts to the news of his son's death in action at sea by smashing the radio set, the new gadget which had captivated the community but which had told lies ranging from faulty weather forecasts to the voice of Lord Haw-Haw. This is the only indication of emotion: the mundane life of crofting and fishing continue and underneath, the grief is absorbed in a kind of primeval dumbness.

The catalogue device is as common in the stories as in the poems, often being employed quite mechanically.[32] If however the device is used not for throwing up an instant framework but in order to gain a distinct narrative point it can of course be fully justified, as in "Tam," "The Story of Jorkel Hayforks" and "The Wheel" in *A Calendar of Love* and "The Whaler's Return" from *A Time to Keep.*

Predominantly, Mackay Brown's story teller is a mediator: the reader is aware of his presence and a distance may be preserved between the reader and the fiction. In the case of the first two stories in the earlier volume ("A Calendar of Love" and "Five Green Waves") and the first two in the later one ("Celia" and "A Time to Keep") this distance closes. If the two pairs are set beside each other a clear advance can be seen. For instance, the over-writing and blurred incantation that mar so much of his weaker writing is still present to a mild degree in the earlier pair. But the focus is distinct: the difficulties and despairs of characters who are seen not as types of Orcadian society but as human beings who happen to be Orcadians. In the second pair this focus is sharper still, the language is spare and the incidental references to the world of the seasons are discreet and pointed. There is a dry precise compassion in "Celia," the story about the girl driven to drink by the thought of the world's cruelty, yet who can respond practically

114

when faced with an immediate case of suffering. The contemporary world may still be viewed from a distance but its effect on her character is crucial and the very distance of its events is relevant to the thematic development of the story. In both "Celia" and "A Time to Keep" there is a concentration of purpose and a focus on living members of a community which are absent not only in many of his short stories and poems but also in his play *A Spell for Green Corn* (1967, pub. 1970) and his novel *Greenvoe* (1972).

*   *   *

Finally, two younger poets whose work clearly belongs to this context are Stewart Conn and Roderick Watson.

Both in its over-all direction and in its handling of tone and rhythm, Conn's work has been more uncertain than one would wish, but there are two characteristics worth comment. The first is his recurrent treatment of childhood memories, located in a distinct Ayrshire milieu, and it is here that his style, when he resists the temptation to make a plain point even plainer, achieves its fullest command of detail and its sharpest focus.

> The shire is sprinkled with his ashes.
> The fields are green through his kind. Their clay,
> His marrow. As much as the roisterer, he: even
> That last ride to Craigie, boots tightly laced,
> His tie held in place by a diamond pin.[33]

Any sense of belonging, however, is meagre. In part this is because the backward gaze is primarily on a private history with few ramifications into a living community. In "On Craigie Hill" he says:

> The land
> Retains its richness—but in other hands.

The farm now belongs to other members of the community but this communal aspect seems to have no place here: the fact that it is now out of the hands of the individual family is sufficient for it to be regarded remotely. In part, too, the poet's own sense of belonging is ambivalent and, despite the loving detail, can seem more a result of will rather than an inescapable compulsion. "On Craigie Hill" ends:

115

> It is hard to look
> Back with any sense of belonging.
> Too much has changed, is still changing.
> This blustery afternoon on Craigie Hill
> I regard remotely the muddy track
> My father used to trudge along, to school.[34]

The second characteristic may appear to have little connection with the first. It is an interest in violence which seems to touch the poet so closely that he has to defend himself from it by distancing: we see it in several tight-lipped poems describing incidents in what appear to be tribal wars in times and places unspecifiably remote.[35] There is butchery, privation, exploitation, fertility-ritual and more butchery. The dry wan language has the effect of highlighting the moments of dismemberment, disembowelling etc, as if these and their fatal attraction were the real and only points of interest in such poems. For all the directness of such moments, they still feel furtive.

There is an interesting blend of these two concerns in "Ayrshire Farm,"[36] a poem which recollects the New Year's Day hare-shoot and then, in two stanzas separated from the first six, recounts a return visit in adulthood to the same scene. The poem ends:

> At the road-end I stopped and stood
> For some time, just listening. My hands
> Growing numb. Then I crossed the track
> To where a single rabbit lay twitching,
> Big-headed, eyes bulging, in pain.
> I took the heaviest stone I could find;
> And with one blow beat in its brains.

The sober unimaginative care with which word is placed by word serves to light up this very fascination in the violence of the action, a fascination which spills over and out of the total context.

It is difficult as yet to see how these characteristics are related and how they can either separately or together enable Conn to deal more sharply with his present continuing environment. The recording of a narrow, personal nostalgia and the depiction of remote violence both seem to entail uneasy restrictions.

So far, the range of reference in Roderick Watson's poetry is

116

much wider. More significantly, he is able to relate this not only to his home locality (Aberdeen) but also to a sense of continuing history, a history in which delicate threads run to and fro between private and family affairs and the broader movements of public history. The verse he has developed for this kind of exploration is of necessity slow-paced and deliberative; it pauses, tests, ruminates, tests again. Obviously it runs the risk of moving too cannily and of being weighed down by an over-anxiety to explain (characteristics we find in both Bruce and Conn when the tension slackens) but when the pace is judged accurately in relation to the details in hand we have a verse which can deal with a considerable meditative range.[37]

"The Constructed Man"[38] recollects a childhood nightmare out of "Mrs Shelley's book"—

>   the constructed man: rises from the box-room
>   his soft and sausage stockinged flesh   roped
>   to walking sticks   trails flex down the stairs
>   descending   in skin coat and rubber boots
>   wrapped in the borrowed envelope of his body
>   and while the fading spark   snaps   within him
>   he gives a smeared   faithful   smile.

But the old horror is not presented as an object for nostalgia: he has his place in the whole history of local, detailed living, and the "we" of verse 6 step on the worn steps like newcomers:

>   We climbed to the old town today.
>   I stood still on the close stairs   rising
>   between many families   the walls scratched
>   and stained by claws and sticks and water
>   wakened at last by the illuminated instant
>   of the bones of your legs   and your buckled shoes
>   so unsteady   walking on broken stones

A connection is then drawn between an acceptance of one's place in these old surroundings and an attempt to welcome the apparition who, despite his dead heart, "reaches out/for remembrance."

Childhood memories are absorbed into a more complex pattern

in "Newsreel."[39] Boyish war-games ("fell for Rommel/at the bottom of the garden") are recalled both fondly and coldly; the real violence outside the cramped false cosiness of the pub continues; and modern technology lets us view these horrors with a nightmarish immediacy which even so may not penetrate our indifference. A sense of disillusion over the very attempt to revivify a belief in the old games is counterpointed against a reluctant but intense observation of the new "real" games. He is afraid of them yet he watches, even if he is the only person in the bar to do so, and he loses sight of the images conveyed by electronic magic simply because the other drinkers obscure his view.

> —to see the play come rouud again: a man in flames
> on television   anonymous as raw meat   prepared
> to burn and doing so for me. When I am not so sure
> of him. Or of him   by the Volkswagen with his fists
> to his ears   facing snowballs thrown by bigger boys
> —the police have already shot him in the chest
> but the shutter is so fast   he doesn't know it yet—
> until his face is lost   among drinkers' backs . . .

Even a sense of helplessness in the face of history is an element of a sense of belonging: a visit to Forvie Sands[40] to inspect a graveyard of the generations who "conspired me here by their various coupling" may be fruitless in that it provides nothing to grasp, yet it affirms the fact of such history ever more strongly without an indulgence in nostalgia or alienation.

> For it is too late to put down all that happened
> here   before my grandmother's family moved to town
> too late to ask the business of those I never knew
> old clothes   faces on a photograph   who pursue
> their yellowed   fading   picnic in the attic
> and not among these stones with half-familiar surnames.

In startling contrast to the Norman knight, with his contrite effigy, is the man operating a model plane on the sands, yet perhaps they do share a kind of celibacy and sense of achievement in that their absorption in a defined activity creates for them a comprehensible reality.

Were the man to stand   say   with his arms apart
he would touch its wings   from tip to tip
in a perfect span — to hold the winter months
of all last year   his hours of patient building.
And that moment of lost time   complete
rigged and fuelled   flew for him today.

Between an immeasurable local history, and an all too measurable
local present, the poet observes: he can register an allegiance to
both without his feelings being seduced by either.

Notes

1. David Black, *L.R. 45* (Summer 1973), pp **48-49**
2. *Stand* (September 1969), pp 9, 15.
3. *Hamlet in Autumn*, pp 18, 45.
4. *Selected Poems*, p. 61.
5. *S.I.R.*, October 1972, p. 26.
6. Edinburgh University Press, 1971.
7. *L.R. 36* (March 1971), p. 39.
8. *C.P.*, p. 8; and David Craig, "A National Literature? Recent Scottish Writing," *Studies in Scottish Literature*, Vol. I, No. 3 (January 1964), p. 158.
9. *C.P.*, pp 57, 85, 110.
10. *C.P.*, p. 11; the passage recurs in "Valediction for 1944," p. 58.
11. *C.P.*, p. 15.
12. *C.P.*, pp 14, 67; cf. pp 17, 19.
13. *C.P.*, pp 2, 4, 77–80.
14. *C.P.*, pp 76, 88, 68.
15. *C.P.*, p. 55.
16. *C.P.*, pp 62–65.
17. *C.P.*, pp 47–48, 71–74; *L.R. 42/43* (October 1972–February 1973), pp 78-81.
18. *L.R. 39* (December 1971) contains *An Rathad Cian/The Far Road* complete, in Thomson's own translation, plus extracts from *Eadar Samhradh is Foghar/ Between Summer and Autumn* (1967) and an introduction by Donald MacAulay. This was also published in book form by New Rivers Press, New York.

19. Donald MacAulay gives an account of these activities in *L.R. 39*. See also Thomson's paper on "The Role of the Writer in a Minority Culture," Transactions of the Gaelic Society of Inverness, XLIV (1964–66), 256–71.

20. BBC Radio 4, 22:3:72.

21. *L.R. 39*, pp 42–43.

22. *Poems New and Selected* (Hogarth, 1971), pp 71, 77, 84, 85, 86, 87, 89, 94.

23. ibid, pp 15, 11.

24. ibid, pp 61, 58, 42.

25. ibid, pp 51–52.

26. *Fishermen with Ploughs* (Hogarth, 1971), p. 27.

27. ibid, pp 73–74.

28. *Poems New and Selected*, p. 87.

29. *Fishermen with Ploughs*, pp 31–32.

30. Gollancz, 1969, pp 28–29, 53, 54, 121, 11.

31. See "The Three Islands," "The Troubling of the Waters," "Master Halcrow, Priest" in *A Calendar of Love* (Hogarth, 1967), and "A Treading of Grapes" in *A Time to Keep* (Hogarth, 1969).

32. See "The Seller of Silk Shirts," "The Ferryman," "Stone Poems" in *A Calendar of Love* and "The Bright Spade" in *A Time to Keep*.

33. "Farm Funeral," *An Ear to the Ground* (Hutchinson, 1972), p. 26.

34. ibid, p. 13.

35. See "Flight," "Outcast," "The Villagers," "Ambush" in *Stoats in the Sunlight* (Hutchinson, 1968); "The Encampment," "Ceremony," "The Hag of the Mill," "Victims" in *L.R. 30* (October 1969); and "The King" in *An Ear to the Ground*; also his play *The King* in Penguin's New English Dramatists No. 14 (1970).

36. *Stoats in the Sunlight*, pp 16–18.

37. For a good and more than unusually compact example see "3 Stones," and for a weaker and unusually diffuse example see "True History on the Walls," both in *Trio: New Poets from Edinburgh* (New Rivers Press, New York, 1971), pp 17, 36–38.

38. *Trio*, pp 21–22.

39. ibid, p. 35.

40. *Spirit* (Summer 1971) (Seton Hall University, New Jersey), pp 62–63.

V

PRIVATE

IN THE WORK OF POETS like George Bruce, Derick Thomson and George Mackay Brown the sense of dependence on and allegiance to a distinct geographical and historical locality is one of the strongest defining characteristics of the poetry. Within the poetry the degree of explicit personal involvement may vary—it is high in Thomson, virtually nil in Mackay Brown—but in each case the overt concern for a particular community is unmistakeable. In contrast, we can group together several other poets who, despite wide individual differences, have it in common that the strongest motivation in their poetry is personal and psychological. They are as poets solitaries in the sense that their work owes little to the kind of communal allegiance already discussed. It is interesting therefore to note that of the five poets grouped here—W. S. Graham, Kenneth White, David Black, Alan Jackson and Alasdair Maclean—only one, Jackson, has spent all his life in Scotland, and, so far as I know, he is also the only one to have expressed any feelings of definite local loyalty: and these were expressed outside his poetry and in a qualified manner.[1] Graham has lived in Cornwall for many years; White has wandered, mainly in France; Black lives in London but has also wandered, to Japan for instance; Maclean has returned to live in Scotland after several years abroad, mainly in Canada.

A few blunt pointers to the areas explored by these poets may be given as follows. Both Graham and White recurrently face the problem of the difficulty and inadequacy of language itself. Even in Graham's most achieved work the *fact* that the obstacle of language is being, hopefully, overcome remains in the foreground. And if White's poetry to date is rather slight it is worth noting here because of his feeling (directly expressed in the poetry) that words are themselves an inadequate medium for the realities he discerns *beyond* words. In Black and Jackson the pattern is more one of search. Black's restlessness takes him through a wide variety of poetic modes, semi-dramatic masks, and temporarily inhabited localities. Jackson's is more static and inward, directed into areas of the subconscious often with the help of Jungian symbols and ideas. In the present context Maclean is particularly interesting since his acute anxieties (about isolation or survival) appear to have found their "objective correlatives" in the landscape and history of his own native region of Ardnamurchan. But his relationship as a poet to this locality is ambiguous and is quite different

123

from, say, Derick Thomson's relationship to Lewis, and for the purposes of the present discussion he belongs firmly to this chapter, not the previous one.

*   *   *

The first of those concerns—the difficulties and inadequacies of language—may indicate a stress which comes close to suffocating the poetry. Much of W. S. Graham's work fights against such a forbidding obstacle and even when it succeeds in avoiding nerveless deliberation and the contortions of metaphorical ellipsis it gains ground only to hold it with considerable strain. Earlier (in a note to Chapter Three) I suggested that the legacy of certain poetic habits developed in the 1940s has had a stifling effect, though these habits are better seen as symptoms rather than a cause. The problem tackled, and his most ambitious attempts to tackle it, can be seen in the title-poems of *The Night Fishing* (1955) and *Malcolm Mooney's Land* (1970).

A central theme of "The Night Fishing" finds its most succinct image here:

> He befriended so many
> Disguises to wander in on as many roads
> As cross on a ball of wool.

The disguises, the selves, the words they use to establish their temporary identities, are all woven together: the dead of night is an image for "the dead of my life," as established in the opening lines, and as finally reaffirmed in the closing lines.

> So I spoke and died.
> So within the dead
> Of night and the dead
> Of all my life those
> Words died and awoke.

The poet's self is a stranger, yet befriended by the sea and welcomed by the present, and it is in this abandonment that he discovers transformation—

> My death
> Already has me clad anew . . .
>
> See how, like an early self, it's loath to leave
> And stares from the scuppers as it swirls away
> To be clenched up . . .

124

> It is myself.
> So he who died is announced. This mingling element
> Gives up myself . . .

In this process of death and rebirth a crucial role is attributed to language though it is never fully clarified.

> The keel in its amorous furrow
> Goes through each word. He drowns, who but ill
> Resembled me . . .

> Now he who takes my place continually anew
> Speaks me thoroughly perished into another . . .

Graham's problem here—how to use the events of the night's fishing as analogues for this process—remains unsolved. The physical and the mental events ought to fuse but too often they remain separate. Part of the reason for this is that the descriptions and the explanations are given to us in different languages. Some of the descriptions have considerable rhythmic power:

> . . . The cross-tree light, yellowing now,
> Swings clean across Orion. And waned and very
> Gently the old signs tilt and somersault
> Towards their home. The undertow, come hard round,
> Now leans the tiller strongly jammed over
> On my hip-bone.

But what happens to the language in lines like these?—

> The illuminations of innocence embrace.
> What measures gently
> Cross in the air to us to fix us so still
> In this still brightness by knowledge of
> The quick proportions of our intricacies?

Only rarely is this kind of allusive precision achieved:

> What one place remains
> Home as darkness quickens?

"Malcolm Mooney's Land" comes nearer to solving a similar problem for now there is less of a disjunction between the description of the polar traveller's isolation and the states of mind explored

125

thereby. The account of the physical situation is not so complete and conclusive; the interpretations are not laid out so explicitly; therefore the two can grow into and out of each other more organically. An element of delirium helps to keep the boundaries ambiguous, as in the phantom presence of "my friend who loves owls" and of "Elizabeth and the boy," and in details such as:

> Yesterday
> I heard the telephone ringing deep
> Down in a blue crevasse.
> I did not answer it and could
> Hardly bear to pass.

Again, language has a crucial role, though now the difficulties of that role are made more explicit. "I urge these words/To find their subtle vents," the narrator says, yet their chances seem slight under "the northern dazzle of silence." He has "reached the edge of earshot."

> Have I not been trying to use the obstacle
> Of language well? It freezes round us all.

Clearly his final isolation is not just geographical: it also seems to be an isolation beyond the possibilities of communication. The poem ends:

> Words drifting on words.
> The real unabstract snow.

Yet the poem itself is there, communicating.

If we look now at the work of the much younger Kenneth White[2] we can see an interesting comparison. Much of White's earlier poetry is too content with routine romantic gestures and unsubstantiated claims ("the deep-down poetry I trade my life for" . . . "I speak in knowledge to all men/the great things and the beautiful I bring"). Where we have a right to expect telling details we are given abstractions. And a sense of immanence is rather glibly contrived by the simple juxtaposition of natural and ecclesiastical imagery. The contrast with *Letters from Gourgounel* is striking, for if we except the more ecstatic passages and make due allowance for the fragmentary nature of the book, we can see his prose there engaging with substantial particular experience much more fully than has been the general rule in his poetry.

Yet there are incidental comments in *Letters* which give a clear indication of the kind of problem he has set himself in his poetry:

> At the moment I am sitting writing at this table, with the great mushroom in my left hand like a torch, trying to give it some eternity. Believe me, I am writing desperately. I do not want to relinquish it. All my writing comes from such wonders, and is the attempt to re-figure them in another element. To transcendentalize them. No phrase is grotesque enough to express what I try to do. (pp. 78–79)

> I stood looking for a while, excited by the sight, despairing at ever incorporating into myself and my writing such a splendour . . . (p. 81)

> . . . I thought of poetry and the idea of poetry flooded into my mind like pure water itself. And I knew there was something in me to keep alive the awareness—something which held the water not like a pitcher, but like the bed of a stream. (pp. 140–41)

Once we begin discussing poetry in these terms it is not easy to discern exactly what we are discussing—but if "poetry" in the sense of a pure essence is envisaged as something too immediate or over-powering to be accurately served by "poetry" in the sense of particular groups of words on a page, then we can see how the inadequacy of White's poetry (in the second sense) originates. The general difficulty is to reconcile the mystic's pull towards wordlessness and the poet's ineradicable dependence upon words. In particular, the poetry's frequent resort to assertion, to statements *about* experience, may be characterised both by abstractions and by a lack of clear focus on such concrete details as are mentioned.

In *The Most Difficult Area* we find White exploring those areas of experience where emptiness and silence may be sensed not in terms of negation but in terms of a more positive approach to a sense of immanence and revelation. "In the Emptiness" seeks to assert, in the emptiness, an experience of "reality right to the bone." In "Beinn Airidh Charr" he refers to such phenomena as

> this light that is
> the limit of austerity
> and makes words blind

And in "At the limits of saying" he returns to the idea of poetry as something which takes over when words leave off:

> at the limits of saying
> the soul flies to the mouth
> and the poem is born

But *what* poem? Is the poem written in words on that particular page a mere preparatory jotting for that other greater poem whose existence we must take on trust?

To what extent White is going to solve that problem in a manner germane to his sensibility remains to be seen, but there are a few short poems which do seem to indicate a possibility. These have clearly learned from oriental models, and their strength is that their focus on details is sharp and their implications are clear without being over-spelt. One of these is "Extraordinary Moment"—

> I have been working all morning
> from midnight till eleven o'clock
>
> now I sit drinking the wine of Maury
> watching the first snow on the mountains
>
> I can describe neither the redness of the wine
> nor the whiteness of the mountains

Another is "Sesshu"—

> After years in China
>
> emptiness achieved
>
> he painted
>
> with the fewest of strokes
>
> the hardness of rocks
>
> the twistedness of roots

But the path seems narrow. While Graham meets his difficulty with poems loaded with substance, White meets his by paring his poems down almost to vanishing point. And the poems are still about poetry/art—moreover, art conceived not as enactment or as exploration but as description. A poet who limits his conception of

128

poetry in this way and whose engrossing interest seems to be in experience beyond language could quite logically stop writing.

*   *   *

David Black's first full collection[3] opens with an executioner's monologue and the executioner's opening remark is:

> Delicacy was never enormously
> My style.

The conscious indelicacy of that first line is characteristic of the delicacy with which Black will calculate his verbal effects. Likewise we are readily struck by the concrete detail through which he seeks to recreate queasy experiences:

> An asym-
> metric spluttering of the
> sluglike
> walls alarmed me . . . [4]

On both counts we detect a much greater pleasure and trust in the efficacy of language than we find in either Graham or White. However elusive Black's "real" self may feel to the reader as it flits ghostily behind the bright facades, there is no denying the clarity and vigour of the relief patterns on the facades.

The inference of a two-dimensional art is not accidental, for the personae which populate much of his earlier work (executioner, eunuch, general, prince, Red Judge, Black Judge, sundry dwarves) make the crude heavily outlined gestures of cartoon characters. And the bizarre horrors, whatever their origin in the poet's inner motivation, are distanced so far into the comic enjoyable area that their demand on the reader's involvement is minimal. Black appears to be making large intricate gestures towards us as a means of remaining himself invisible. Certainly the grotesque possibilities are relished: the absurd version of extrovert v. introvert in "An Epic of Self-Discovery," perhaps betrayed by the studied casualness of "One's intestines are always unnerving." Or the *reductio ad absurdum* of "My Species," about the (prime?) minister whose sperm was separated out in order to produce 5 million infants. Or the hectic inevitability of "The Fury was on me," with its less than reluctant victim:

129

> (I foresaw that the breadbin could become an embarrassment,
> But there was no escape, and to be truthful
> I'm glad to attract attention, rather than not.)

For all Black's skill in recreating this slithery logic of dream, he leaves unsolved the considerable problem of how dream-material *can* be directly used in poetry. A dream may have a coherent logic but can still rest on meaningless premises: for the reader the only satisfactory clues exist in the connections the poet himself indicates between the dream and non-dreaming life. The fact that a psychiatrist (and Black is, incidentally, interested in Jungian analysis) could perhaps provide some clues, after the event, is another possibility altogether.

The semi-dramatic nature of many of these early personae lead naturally to attempts at more fully narrative types of poem, and some of Black's more interesting (if less patently successful) work has explored various possibilities of embodying a story-line without sacrificing the close-packed detail of effect more typical of short poems. *With Decorum* contains two examples—"Without Equipment" (six pages) and "A Rite of Spring" (fifteen pages). The first concerns the search for a missing and irreplaceable ball from a juggling set.

> What
> is your mission whistle
> the grunting pipes, and as he gulps at a
> fluent
> slobber the whole
> room con-
> vulses and recovers shaking. I am
> here in search, I say, of a wooden
> ball.

The second describes a feverish mother-search-and-rescue operation: the mother is found, but eaten during pursuit by ravenous ant-monsters.

> There are parts of one's life, how-
> ever significant, too
> corny for treatment. Tell me about your
> mother.

Since there seem to be few bounds set to the corniness of treatment, we can take this remark as an instance of the studied casualness already mentioned: this is a common enough feature of fantasy-writing but it can defeat its purpose rather easily.

In both poems the proliferation of detail carries more interest than the overall narrative. As in dreams, these details may be visualised with a hallucinatory clarity, yet the connections between them and their underlying significance can remain nebulous. In terms of poetic structure, there is often little reason why a particular tendril should start or stop growing where it does.

The first and most substantial section of *The Educators* offers four other and different attempts at narrative. The narrative surface of the title poem is explicit and the piece generally is tied up in a manner which is not typical of his more characteristically allusive work. In this case the fable of the educators who tear the dwarf apart would have gained in significance if we had been told more about the educators and their motives: as it is, the simple contrast between their sudden violent attack and their customarily sober and ordered behaviour has the nature of a cliché. "Tancred Restored" on the other hand relates back to some of the less explicit narratives in *With Decorum*. The suggestions are made more densely than in the first poem: in this case a more explicit narrative would have helped to give them a more clearly realised direction. One of the basic problems of narrative poetry is the question of how much narrative reference must be given; and, in giving it, what advantages can you wring from the fact that you are not using functional prose? The second two poems in this group illustrate two kinds of answer. In "Document of an Inter-Stellar Journey" we are given a series of tiny extracts and we can imply for ourselves the underlying narrative. Clearly this method is one of the most useful for building up a poem with a narrative structure, but it is doubtful if this narrative contains enough development to justify the poem. This might not have mattered if some of the suggestions hinted at *en route* had been taken up, as from an item like:

> vast wilderness. Even the blast
> a
> thread, in that stagnant ocean

"Anna's Affairs," however, offers a very full narrative.[5] The action is reduced to a primal level and further character development would have been irrelevant. Although the narrator announces at the start that his "concern is the blank business of chronicling" and although the comparative austerity of much of the detail bears out this concern, the chronicle is interlaced with the narrator's comments. These may take the form of asides, as when he catches himself in the role of envious peeping-tom: "Absurd aspiration/in the straight string that would wish to be knotted!" Or they may take the form of a remark straight from narrator to reader: "Let me not/weary the daylights out of you with/two further repetitions." What has been gained or obscured by not writing the lines as prose is doubtful. For instance would the verbal manners of the following lines risk an appearance of preciosity if they were set as prose and were thus read within a different context of expectations? Here they are as prose:

> I find how she terms me. The dwarf my brother. There is a flashy combination of catcalls. It is perhaps local in time merely: we are currently barely speaking: said with horrible venom just the same. I was in a pine-tree, several branches above where the tall man spikes his linen; and heard their exchanges.

Now as divided into lines:

> I find how she terms me. The dwarf my brother. There is a
>   flashy combination of catcalls. It is perhaps
> local in time merely: we are
> currently barely speaking: said with
> horrible venom just the same. I was in a pine-tree,
> several branches above where the tall man spikes his linen; and
> heard their exchanges.

The third part of *The Educators* raises, in a shorter compass, very similar questions to those raised in the first part. Here we have sixteen short poems presented with the over-all caption "Poems from *Autobiography*" as if their variegated and fragmentary nature were due to the fact that they are extracted from a bigger whole. Whether the context of this whole, if it exists, would give more cohesion to the separate parts we have no means of knowing. In the meantime the cohesion to be gathered merely from the implication of the caption is slight, largely because of the variety of the modes explored. For instance, at the furthest remove from reporting we

132

have a kind of miniature myth-making (No. 2). In contrast Nos. 5 and 13 describe events from a very close range: if we are meant to feel that those events are significant, we simply have not been shown how. The history of a finished friendship (No. 9) is by its nature more amenable to recall and comment. Again, in No. 11, events observed but not necessarily involving the narrator personally are more readily objectified.

Clearly in terms of craftsmanship Black's work has an adventurousness, energy and clarity of presentation that marks him off from his contemporaries. Yet this does not necessarily entail a more open commitment either to the underlying significance of his material or indeed to the reader. Without, I hope, risking an argument *ad hominem* it is possible to see his variegated poetic performances as a mode of avoiding such commitment: as if they were incidental happenings of a pilgrimage. Although Black is more committed to the power of words (and more skilful in their use) than White, we do find, particularly in more recent work, references to areas of moral concern in which we can well imagine the games of syllables and masks being laid aside as a frivolity, and these references are comparable in their implications for the poetry to White's admissions of the inadequacies of his medium. A recent group of fourteen poems concludes with this one called "Theology"—

> Once a doll made of salt (said Ramakrishna)
> went to measure the depth of the mighty ocean.
> O the echoing, surging waves accepted it—

Another poem, "September," from the middle of the set, ends:

> Let me not forget that God e-
> xists as master of *maya* and not otherwise.
> Yet the glib formulations do not close the
> issue, which is expressed in days and weeks of
> sun and squall and the skies that hurry for no man;
> and transferred into words, evaporates, or
> makes a poem or two, no doubt, and things of that sort—[6]

Yet this is paradoxical ground, since the most powerful use of words often arises in spite of a realisation of their inadequacy (*vide* Iain Crichton Smith) so the question should be left open.

At least we can be certain that the sense of belonging to a

particular locality and community—such as we see in Derick Thomson—has little place in the shifting scenes of Black's work. The "autobiographical" section of *The Educators* is headed by this quotation:

> . . . the mindful exert themselves; to no abode are they attached; like swans that quit their pools, home after home they abandon.
>
> *Dhammapada*, 91.

As a justification for the fragmentary nature of that section this is clearly inadequate, just as clearly as he wants to make the gesture, in someone else's words to boot. There is a similar gesture in "Tho His Name is Well-known," one of the short poems in the middle section of *The Educators*, and here again the distancing is achieved through the use of a persona (Rumpelstiltskin) which may allow us not to take the gesture too seriously. Rumpelstiltskin is condemned to perpetual wandering:

> knowing nothing
> but his name   his riddle
>
> that every passer
> answers correctly

There is an interesting comment on this homeless freedom in the first poem of the same section (i.e. Part Two of *The Educators*). "Ruins" is about his own attempts to make things: he distinguishes himself from the "lover of artifice" who can build "finished structures," for his allegiance is to the "vast/unfinished unlimited/web of causes," he works "wrenched in confusion" and produces "these ruins." The structure of the poem is itself almost ruinous, with irregular lines, wrenched grammar and sheer deliberate awkwardness. In what sense are we to take this careful artificer's dissociation from artifice? In what sense are we to understand his allegiance to "the vast/unfinished unlimited/web of causes" as a central motivation in his creation of artifices? Could it account for the fragmentary and ruinous nature of much of his work, however "finished" in detail much of it is? Yet contrast "Ruins" with the last poem in the section, "It was love"—

> In a great draught the window
> sucks at the flowered curtain
> then releases

134

I lie bent, fully clothed, in the harsh light
gaze on white walls
the clock is loud, like speech

"it was love.
I must have wanted
to destroy it"

On the few occasions when Black does attempt a simple statement
of this kind, in which we *can* sense an open personal commitment
both to his own experience and to the reader, the contrast with the
general tenor of his work is startling. In neither "Ruins" nor "It
was love" do we have personae: yet the extent to which we can
trust the first person pronoun is another open question.

* * *

In contrast to the variegated modes and personae of Black's
poetry, Alan Jackson's work may appear monolithic: one relatively
constant tone of voice, one dominant area of investigation, and a
restricted range of formal habits. His views of poetry are heart-felt,
readily expressed, yet nebulous. Three typical utterances will
illustrate. The first is the negative part of his response to the Carcanet
Press survey *British Poetry since 1960*:

> This is a book that by negatives tells you where to go. It is a book
> that tells you to be diffident, scrupulous, modest, hesitant,
> accurate, critical, wary, unambitious, rational, complex, con-
> cerned, worried, relevant, competent, tentative, restrained,
> democratic, quiet, objective. This book is made of concrete and
> glass; it is written with white chalk on a white board; it is
> the articulated mumblings of the suburban-welfare-agnostic-
> pensionable-academic-consensus of terribly hard-working well-
> meaning terrified egos. This book is pre-Einstein, pre-Nietszche
> precooked and post-mortem . . . a book largely by and for the
> salaried technicians of poetry. Courage, truth and love were not
> mentioned: only technique, accuracy and relevance. It was not
> about poetry in the sixties.

The other two are from "The Knitted Claymore," an essay which
combined personal credo and polemical attack on certain aspects
of Scottish life and letters.

135

Some men one can agree and disagree with calmly; mutual areas of difference are maintained and respected. Others give themselves totally to one vision, one cause, and boast of their dedication. All facts feed it, everything must be related to it; they give no quarter; their world finally becomes divided into friends (few) and enemies (many). That they do most harm to themselves is true, but the world turns too fast and is too crowded for that to be our first consideration. The question is that they are dangerous both in politics and art. They have the power of creation, or at least of writing, but they use it to make dark rather than light . . .

. . . the only "Scottish" writer who has largely altered me and so is part of my tradition is A. S. Neill . . . it is mainly foreign thinkers who've had their way with me—Tolstoy, Nietzsche, Spengler, Jung, Sartre and Camus, Norman Mailer, Laurens van der Post. And beyond the horizon there is Eastern wisdom which I allow to exert a gently correcting pressure on the two main influences which affect us all, those embodied in the figures of Christ and Faust . . . The works of Jung have been the main influence in my life since I was twenty . . . [7]

The moral absolutism, with its plea for openness as against constrictive sectarian loyalties, the polemical vigour and impatience, and the gallant propensity to plunge into deep water are all characteristic features of his thinking which strongly influence the direction of his poetry. If, as polemics, such remarks are more sharply defined *contra* rather than *pro*, we have to look in the poetry for the substance of his plea, and here we are in admittedly obscure regions—

> of course mythologies wonders and gloom.
> how else can we talk?[8]

For his one dominant area of investigation—the self—is not presented with an explicit autobiography: the pilgrimage may be inwards, but into the archetypal universal self which, hopefully, we all share. In such a case the poet commits himself to the possibility that in reporting on his own inner mythologies, wonders and gloom he can enable the reader to find common ground within himself.

The subconscious hinterland of private and communal dreams and of recurring fables is therefore invitingly accessible. The title

136

poem of *The Grim Wayfarer*[9] for instance has many of the elements associated with traditional Christian allegory. The wayfarer follows "the steepest path through the woods;" he leads his followers into the wasteland; he doesn't eat for forty nights; his followers die off and he is left alone, to suffer a period of negation (a dark night of the soul, a cloud of unknowing):

> Hold out your pitcher and it will have the bottom broken.
> Knock and the door will disappear. Seek, and you will be turned blind.

Then comes revelation as "a flish flash of light out of the sky" and renewal in the form of a child. On his entry to the wilderness he had surrendered his heart as a kind of passport, but he is now warned not to stop for it on his return:

> Those who have it think they have you. Let them. They have catalogued and filed you. You are numbered and dead, as their counting goes. This is an asset.

The wayfarer returns, dead to the world and singing. The tauter verse of the song which concludes the poem contrasts with the looser prose of the main section, but it is doubtful if the latter is the right and final form for the material. This kind of dream/myth narrative can obsess a writer with its possible meanings but can yet remain curiously outside language: it can resist the writer stubbornly and often he can do little more than jot it down in note form. However this volume—his one main collection to date—would have been poorer without this poem because it points to a general context within which many of the other poems have a place.

In "Siren trouble," for example, the narrator/wayfarer is at the mercy of natural inclinations, immersed in carnal delights but not without a sense of unease:

> there's something at the back of my mind
> that used to be at the front.

"End," hovering on the edge of coherence, admits:

> i'm built on rot
> and shiftiness

137

and protests against the impending negation by listing various ways of having or not having a recognisable or desirable identity. "Hero trek," about an ultimate encounter, stresses the treacherous uncertainties in which the hero must act decisively ("in the mud world," "where mist meets fog," "the octopus sludge"). The tribulations of the personal quest are related to the desires and desperations of groups ("The tribe") and humanity at large ("Three little green quarters"). "The Duke of Ire," with a more consciously elaborated allegory, seeks to hold together both individual and historical levels of interpretation. The prelapsarian couple, knowledge of whom makes the duke fret, have their nest somewhere in the labyrinthine basement areas of the castle: he is at the top, which is now five hundred feet high through the storey-by-storey additions of his ancestors. He lacks the technical means of further arithmetical, upward development, and his dilemma is presented strongly but obscurely as a contemporary one:

> I'm not an evil man
> I live completely
> off what I grow here
> it's just the knack
> I've got
> of knowing what's what
> and acting acc.
> that makes me touchy
> and not well liked
>
> . . .
>
> and three choices
> between here and not building
> or up and on and out
> or down
> which I'd never heard was
> a direction
> up till now

Generally the narrator is not exactly a dramatic persona—he is simply "i." Now and then "i" may appear as an individual frustrated by his failures ("Digging"), hurt by the insolence of those less well endowed but more numerous ("Person"), impatient at the numbing effects of tolerance and easy-going ("Notice"). But "i" is also an all-purpose protean factor:

> i am bent with sign-posts
> i am a mirror fan
> i am plagued by creeps
> by the worried furrowed lines
> of knitting myself together
> which makes me sick
> but a little dry sick
> not a bloody coloured eruption ("End")

By the old analogy of *sicut interius et exterius*, there are few limits to what "i" can accommodate.

> only one city
>   and it's guarded
> only one guard
>   and it's self
> only one self
>   it's divided
>   ("And did those feet")

> i have my own most internal
> dramatics most theatrical
> innards . . .

> the beast and bastardy that comes along
> with the nine pound brain and opposable thumb
> of man . . .   ("Tonite")[10]

"i" can be a black hollow, can search out another "i"—

> Am your person at the door. Black hollow waits. Have
> you light there for me to steal like sweetness?
> Or will you open from darkness too, all glum,
> expecting me to flood you up with good?
> Do I have to be the sun to make love? A god
> to fill you? Your female dark's my too great
> need, but if you're waiting so for me, and God!
> both failing, then Christ! how lost in wants, us,
> from each other . . .

139

> . . . If I have the strength not to knock on,
> will you have the strength not to open,
> that shadow-locked, complaining, mutual, delusive door?

("Wallowbaby Playtime: Finis")[11]

The exploratory nature of such writing clearly demands from the poet considerable respect for the raw material he shapes: the images are often by their very nature and by their subconscious origin blurred with significances. Were they sharp-edged they would be more amenable to rigorous shaping. As it is, the imposition of an intellectually devised order could be destructive. But this leads to two problems which are as yet unresolved in Jackson's work, and perhaps, given the nature of his talents, he is unwilling or unable or sees no need to solve them. The first affects the central area of his work, for his perceptions here tend to crystallise into small units, either within longer poems or as short poems in their own right.[12] Except where he occasionally uses the narrative framework of a fable, then, his longer poems, such as "End" or "And did those feet," or more exactly those of his poems which extend further than a few short paragraphs, depend on connections which often remain quite hidden from the reader. The very present sense of manipulating difficult or recalcitrant material is doubtless maintained but often at considerable expense to the logic of his utterance. The strong but not very flexible rhythm, especially when combined with a catalogue structure, can be used to bounce the poet (and hopefully the reader?) over some very opaque patches.

The second problem is more peripheral and it rises at the more polemical moments when spiritual or physical enemies are scented. Here the preacher intervenes, and the preacher does not explore— he simplifies and asserts. And the more he does so, the vaguer the target becomes and the softer the blow. Man the Brute ("The Worstest Beast") is such a hulk you can hardly miss. Arithmetical Man clearly irritates the poet, appearing in "Three little green quarters," "Falling" and "The Newton Man." And the Liberal or Intellectual Man is another windmill:

> well i am guilty and that is reaction
> by the liberal light
> well i am humble and there's treason
> to the liberal light

> well i need, i bleed, and that's heresy
>   to the upstander intellect
>   ("Renegade Mechanego")[13]

Defensive gestures, clearly, but against whom and in defence of what?

There can be no doubting the sense of personal commitment in Jackson's poetry: it is more obvious than in the work of any of the other poets so far discussed in this chapter. It is sufficiently pronounced at times to be the principal concern of the poetry, thus determining both its strengths and its restrictions.

> i say that i'm stuck in a mirror
>   that melts into a swamp.
>   ("He says that he's stuck")

A tenuous control seems to be accepted over the incidence of sharp reflections and their vanishing into muddy waters which may, for all we at times are allowed to know, be deep or shallow.

*　*　*

On an obvious level the poetry of Alasdair Maclean is rooted in his native locality of Ardnamurchan yet his poetic use of the features of that locality marks him off sharply from the sense of belonging to a particular way of life which characterises the work of such poets as Derick Thomson, George Bruce and George Mackay Brown. At the same time he offers some sharp contrasts with those Scottish poets whose local background plays a relatively insignificant role and whose poetry is more directly influenced by personal psychological pressures. Whatever prior difficulties he may or may not experience in the making of his poems, there is no sense of language as such being an obstacle or an inadequate tool, whereas in W. S. Graham and Kenneth White respectively such feelings become an integral part of the substance of the poetry. When Maclean, within a poem, refers to his writing he does so in the matter-of-fact way of a craftsman. Yet he does not share David Black's willingness to experiment in various modes, for his style is avowedly plain, that of an unhurried speaking voice which knows what it is talking about: a steadiness which can make Black's personae, for all their more subtle articulations, appear restless and shifting. Again, this plain manner sets him at a distance from Alan Jackson's willingness to present the reader with opaque

141

statements which *feel* significant but may not be. Whatever psychological pressures shape Maclean's poems—and the evidence in the poems indicates that they are strong—he clarifies his intentions to the extent of giving his readers a firm hold at the very first reading.

Granted, such remarks as this—

> I suppose that my attitude to conservation is about the same as I would have if I were drowning in the sea and someone threw me a plastic lifebuoy. I wouldn't consider it a practicable alternative to throw it back and demand a genuine cork one. I would let myself be dragged reluctantly ashore.[14]

—such a remark may well remind us of some of Derick Thomson's poems on similar topics ("High Summer," "Donald Cam, My Boy"). And in some of the poems themselves, such as "Highland Castle" and "At the Peats,"[15] we find the cold knowledgeable disenchantment of the highlander who stares back at the intruder, whether the latter has come to improve or just to take snap-shots. "Highland Castle" however hints at a dissociation one would not expect in a whole-hearted local commitment:

> I've taken a more solitary path since then
> and what the separation costs me
> is my own affair.

This links up with one of the most explicit statements Maclean has made about his poetry:

> My poems are an eye-witness account, a personal testimony. This is me standing up among my own people to be counted. But I hope, too, that these poems are more than that. I hope that they are testimony in a wider sense. I believe the wilderness to be where the human spirit draws its strength from, where the imagination has its source, where the images come from. I think that if you destroy the wilderness, as we are now doing, you also remove those possibilities. I think the result will be a generation or two of urban poetry and then silence.[16]

Two points are worth noticing here. First, the eye-witness account is only in part concerned with "my own people" because in the most intensely felt of his poems what he gives us is personal rather than communal testimony. In such poems he takes from his own locality and its way of life such material as will act as objective imagery for the exploration of his own concerns. Second, the

142

wilderness he refers to is not only the geographical one of the north-west highlands: it is also a spiritual wilderness. Here too, as much as in the parallel physical wilderness, is a source of imaginative strength.

The sign-posts he offers us have, as statements, a crisp simplicity, and yet the areas of experience to which they refer may be difficult. Take these two ideas:

> A bleak, inhuman, fearful landscape:
> something to roll up and stow in my mind
> against those odd moments of happiness.
>
> ("View from my Window")

> While the days swagger, elbow one another,
> I wait, with what sadness I can muster.
> This white weather doesn't suit me,
> I think. I get fatter all the time.
> For weeks I live off my stored darkness.
>
> ("I Hate Midsummer in the North")[17]

We would normally think of storing up happiness and light against moments of sorrow and bleakness, and this fearful distrust of the obvious sources of common health and joy recurs in "Thoughts after Rain," one of the few poems with autobiographical reference outside Scotland. Referring to his experience of India he says:

> It was the first time ever I regretted
> my contact with the surface of the world.
> I feared to catch up on my sleep by day
> lest I should lie down flat and wake up curled.[18]

The motif of self-preservation is pronounced. He spells it out less cryptically in "Hedgehogs and Geese," where he compares the reaction of both species to the onset of winter. Despite his momentary envy of the geese—"a moment lecherous for height/and uncorrupted space"—he accepts the earth-bound home-bound conditions:

> But that's the vision unbraced by the will
> or the spirit premature as usual.
> At heart no flyer
> I bristle timidly when touched.
> When the ice comes I retreat beneath it.
> I choose at last hedge-hogs.[19]

Writing too seems to be an element, and an important one, in this process of survival. In "October," as "Darkness closes in. Or spreads out," both animals and poet look to their defences.

> Something is already nibbling
> at the edges of the field
> in which my cottage stands,
> swallowing the grass,
> leaving the rocks
> at the side of its plate.
> I write, nevertheless.[20]

More oblique references, which act as pin-points or jabs at the reader, reinforce this cumulative pressure. Nerves, for instance— "your peeled nerves would curl to the screams of cut flowers " or, as a definition of a scream, "two nerve-ends being rubbed together." Or wounds, like his grandfather's fatal gash in the throat—

> He was trying so hard to say something
> the red lips under his chin
> grinned and wagged with the effort . . .

or the shot-gun wounds on the man whose efforts to kill himself proved clumsy and protracted:

> When he looked down at his belly
> he saw a dozen tiny mouths
> all with thin lips primly clamped together.

Or rats, either by themselves in an abandoned house

> Don't worry about rats.
> Of any colony that existed
> there will be only one survivor.
> It will be too fat to move.

—or as an image forcing itself upon the poet at a moment of crisis. He recalls seeing a friend who had died of TB:

> You were no friend of mine.
> You looked like a rat then, Willie
> and you gnawed your way into my brain.

144

And he relates a feeling of terror at the prospect of a committed personal relationship to a method of killing rats by trapping them in wire cages and then lowering the cages into water.[21] Indeed, man-woman relationships in these poems tend generally to be harsh, predatory or zoological.[22]

A basic question which now rises concerns how Maclean's poetry handles the psychological pressures which it attempts to meet and direct. His own description of his writing, made with reference to a nineteenth century preacher, takes us only so far.

> His rule of thumb
> for preaching is the one I use to write:
> "a plain statement of the marvellous
> and a marvellous statement of the plain."[23]

This is true enough as an indication of a tone of voice and of a general attitude of respect for the material in hand. But, as is clear from the quotations, the points of immediate pressure in the verse are met by a corresponding sharpness of definition, and at those points the statement is least plain, depending for its marvellous effect on often surprising similes and metaphors. Naturally, not all similes and metaphors in Maclean's poetry register crucial points: they can occur as incidental bonuses as in the work of any poet (such as MacCaig) with an eye for playful correspondences. In "Squall"[24] a small cloud comes up at the edge of a blue sky "like an anarchist peering over a garden wall;" the poem is not without serious possibilities—

> Resistance is a necessity for squalls
> and this one duly went to look for it

—though crucial questions of the poet's own response do not arise. On the other hand they can rise in an ambiguous form when the similes and metaphors introduce connotations which jar against or even trivialise their context. "Three-legged Frog" is about a frog who has almost lost one of its back legs through being caught by a scythe and refers to the mutilated lurching animal as "a traveller with an empty suitcase." In "Death of a Hind" the half-killed animal is compared to "a stage drunk going round a lamppost."[25] Perhaps a shock effect is intended, but this does not rule out the possibility of the marvellous statement betraying the plain truth of the feelings.

Effect, of a theatrical and Hitchcock type, is an important element in several poems whose basic development consists of listing variations on a simple idea, usually entailing a hallucinatory exaggeration and distortion of everyday perceptions—"Tests for Aloneness," "Some Rules for Visiting an Abandoned House," "On Holiday in Ardnamurchan," "The Roar," and "Things get Heavier."[26] We may feel that the underlying fear, menace and isolation in such poems need not be taken too seriously in view of the relish in the neat performance. But shouldn't they? "Bathrooms: A Few Definitions" ends like this:

> They are where one day your vision clears for good.
> You can see through the man in the mirror.
> You can see the sadness depositing inside his heart.
> You can see the shelf in his mind where the razor is kept.[27]

We may indeed wonder what intense anxieties *are* being half-revealed, half-concealed by the crisp statements. Certainly these poems contrast sharply with the conventional method, not common in Maclean, of using an analogy (e.g. with a storm) simply to assert a personal predicament. He does this in "Wild Night"—"I have fired my last flare./All I can do now is hold on."—without letting us into the circumstances which make him feel like this.[28]

On the other hand the possibilities open to Maclean's verse do include a more objective handling of both topographical and social material from his own region. It is objective to the degree that the points of personal pressure do not impinge directly upon the reader, at the immediate surface level: if the harsh material, hard rock and hard emotion, acts as an "objective correlative" for the poet then that in one sense is his business, though in another sense it could be a measure of the poetry's success. Whichever way, the objectivity of such poems is qualified by a highly selective process, and the voice is far from being that of a communal spokesman.

One of the most interesting recent examples of such poems is "Stone,"[29] a set of five pieces. The central three are about some of the past inhabitants of this rocky environment. Part II describes a fight in 1868 between two men: the victor, having annihilated his victim's head, is accused of having pebbles hidden in his hands:

146

His fists, they found, had locked shut; fists no more
but lumps of stone. The parish record says
they had to break his fingers to get them open.

Part III begins:

"From stone you came," said the preacher, "and to stone
you shall return. Stone you must be all your days.
Come, let me chisel you!"

This preacher's ministry, in 1800, was unconventional, popular, but,
since judged heterodox by the authorities, short-lived. The section
ends with the poet's nod of agreement, already quoted: it implies both
that the poet may have a function in such a community but that,
given the context here, it may be an uneasy one. A personal connection is also made in Part IV, this time through a sketch of the poet's
grandfather, whose very longevity has a stony quality. "His soft
coevals fell away, destroyed by love," whereas he, when at last he
took to his bed, never had "the least crack in him." Parts I and V
frame those three central parts in their landscape—the rock which
seems to have entered their souls. "God was short of earth when
he made Ardnamurchan"—so, in a phrase that characteristically
blends an apparent surprising reversal and simple literal truth,
Maclean relates how "there were three houses cropped from one
field." Part V refers this landscape to its people in a way that
opens out the time scale geologically: with no soft ground the choice
for burying places was between the bog and the beach. Fearing the
preservative qualities of the bog, they chose the beach. The three
varying conclusions are worth quoting. First, the version printed
in *The Listener:*

They chose the beach and there they are today
under the short turf. The wind plays archaeologist.
Their bones project at silly angles, break
and are crunched underfoot. New sand, new possibilities.

Then the version printed in *Lines Review:*

They chose the beach and there they are today
under the short turf. No stone below and none above,
only a weight of sand and the wind slowly easing it.

147

The removal of the "archaeologist" personification and of the over-stressed description of the protruding bones, "at silly angles" and "crunched underfoot," and the abandonment of the all-too-open and magnanimous "possibilities" all serve to focus our attention less distractedly on the bare physical facts yet thereby to intensify our realisation of the implications. Our response to "easing" ranges from the recognition of a simple fact through a shiver (the bones will be exposed) to an apprehension of its ambiguities: we have here both the ease of death itself and the suggestion that the landscape even in death weighs uncomfortably on its inhabitants.

With such considerations in mind we may contemplate the version which was finally printed in *From the Wilderness:*

> They chose the beach and there they are today
> under the short turf. No stone within a mile of them,
> only the weight of time and the wind's slow curiosity.
> I could wish my own bones, when I hand them back,
> so soft a bed, so sweet and cool a resurrection.

Notes

1. *L.R. 37* (June 1971), p. 3.

2. *The Cold Wind of Dawn* (Cape, 1966), *Letters from Gourgounel* (Cape, 1966), *The Most Difficult Area* (Cape Goliard, 1968).

3. *With Decorum* (Scorpion Press, 1967). This was followed by *The Educators* (Barrie and Rockliff, 1969) and *The Happy Crow* (Lines Review Editions 4, 1974).

4. *With Decorum*, pp 36–37.

5. See also the similar techniques of "Peter MacCrae Attempts The Active Life," *The Happy Crow*, pp 9–21.

6. *L.R. 42/43*, pp 77, 75. This set of poems (pp 71–77), an elaborate constellation of variegated references and modes, is an apt illustration both of the variety of Black's work and of the elusiveness of any committed personal points of reference. They are ordered differently in *The Happy Crow*.

7. *S.I.R.*, November 1972; *L.R. 37*, pp 10–11, 26, 28.

8. "He says that he's stuck," *S.I.R.*, March 1973, p. 25.

9. Fulcrum, 1969. Poems referred to and not otherwise documented are from this collection.

10. *L.R. 33* (July 1970), pp 17–18.

11. *L.R. 47* (Winter 1973), p. 35.

12. See for instance the third verse of "The Caves;" or the short poem "an animal walks . . ." in *The Grim Wayfarer*, pp 21 and 29.

13. *S.I.R.*, March 1973, p. 21.

14. *Listener* 7:12:72, p. 777.

15. *L.R. 30* (October 1969), p. 6 and *From the Wilderness* (Gollancz, 1973), p. 10.

16. *Listener*, as above, p. 776.

17. *From the Wilderness*, pp 41, 30.

18. ibid, pp 21–22.

19. ibid, p. 53.

20. *L.R. 30*, p. 17.

21. "The Roar," "Screams," "My Grandfather's Razor," *L.R. 30*, pp 6, 11–12, 9–10; "A Death in the Family" and "Some Rules for Visiting a Deserted House," *From the Wilderness*, pp 38–40, 15–16; "To Willie Robertson: Dead of Consumption" and "Question and Answer," *L.R. 30*, pp 10, 7.

22. As well as "Question and Answer" see "The Agents," "Things Get Heavier," and "Pigeons," *L.R. 30*, pp 7, 14, 15. One notable exception is "Fiona with a Fieldmouse," *New Edinburgh Review* (November 1969), p. 31 and in *Spirit* (Seton Hall University, N.J., Summer 1971), p. 34: Fiona is a child but the possibilities for her future happiness as a wife and mother are entertained positively and tenderly.

23. "Stone," Part III, *From the Wilderness*, pp 12–13.

24. *L.R. 30*, p. 16.

25. *From the Wilderness*, pp 32, 35.

26. *L.R. 30*, pp 3, 5, 6, 14; *From the Wilderness*, p. 15.

27. *S.I.R.*, August 1971, p. 32.

28. *From the Wilderness*, p. 20.

29. The slightly differing versions are in *L.R. 42/43*, pp 127–29; *Listener*, as above, pp 778–79; and *From the Wilderness*, pp 11–14.

VI

LINGUISTIC

ANY SIMPLE STATEMENT about "English and Scots" poetry within an overall Scottish context has to be immediately qualified. On an elementary level the orthographic differences may suggest a greater divide than is really the case. An outsider, for instance, browsing through MacCaig and Garioch, will see certain differences at once: but should he hear them reading he will recognise both voices as distinctly Scottish—indeed they both reflect facets of the self-same Edinburgh. MacCaig's voice, both literally and as the controlling voice of his poetry, is at a far remove from so-called Received English, that homeless esperanto which is *received* only by media licence holders and EFL pupils but which *gives* nothing in terms of a local and individual voice which can be exploited poetically. On a less elementary level the differences clearly felt between Scottish poetry in Scots and Scottish poetry in English have not proved very susceptible to rational argument. The customary observations that the English-writing Scottish poet uses English "with a Scottish accent" or that he shows his Scottishness "in other ways" beg more questions than they answer; they rest on assumptions one is still free to trust or distrust.

Again, the use of the word "dialect" in this context can be sensitive. For polemical purposes it is regularly asserted that Scots is not a dialect but a "national language," an assertion denoting strength of feeling rather than any attempt to meet the basic question: to what extent *is* Scots a distinct language rather than a group of residual dialects? It is certainly not a complete language, either geographically or in terms of its actual range of usefulness. Geographically, the varieties that make up Lowland Scots belong to the Borders, the Central Lowlands and northwards up the east coast into Aberdeenshire, the latter area retaining considerable richness. But this is only part of Scotland and if we look at it from the spacious west, north-west and north, it looks rather a small part. The Gaelic-English divide, patently a very clear one, is now open to sympathetic and rational discussion on many sides; but the very closeness of English and Scots, like the love-hate between near relatives, helps to perpetuate spiky and restrictive attitudes.

In its range of use—its actual everyday range as distinct from its historical or potential future—Scots is also limited. Here a second basic question rises: to what extent are those dialects so limited in their expressive range that they have to be supplemented by usages culled from dictionaries? One of the characteristics of Scots verse, as in Garioch, is an ability to move between the colloquial and the bookish, but if the latter element becomes more and more indispensable this balance of forces is no longer possible. At a general level it is a matter of "roots" and a "living language," but more particularly it is simply a matter of vocabulary: for instance a dialect that reflects a basically rural or artisan way of life would have to develop beyond recognition before becoming an adequate tool for, say, scientific speculation. Thus we can question the sense in which certain Scottish writers claim to be "bilingual." The bilingualism of a Gaelic-English writer such as Iain Crichton Smith is of a sharper kind. And if we think of someone who moves freely between French and German, or Hungarian and Russian, we have a case of involvement in two languages both of which are complete, a situation radically different from that of the writer in Scots. Again, if we think of more extreme instances of poets crossing linguistic barriers, such as Ondra Lysohorsky or Paul Celan, any Scots writer's claim to bilingualism becomes virtually meaningless.

To go no further back than a couple of decades, it is incontrovertible that the bulk of the most important Scottish poetry has been written in English. If we list a range—Edwin Morgan, Iain Crichton Smith, Norman MacCaig, George Bruce, George Mackay Brown, Alasdair Maclean, Alan Jackson, David Black—it is obvious that a similar range of Scots-writing poets does not exist. In some quarters there is reluctance to accept this fact, evident for instance in the over-rating of inferior work simply because it is in Scots. Yet it would be unfair to attribute this reluctance merely to base chauvinism. It stems, at best, from a knowledge and love of a rich tradition and from a more general realisation that any lapsing or desuetude of a mode of expressing a particular consciousness is a human loss. It is understandable that any piece of evidence which argues against such diminishment should be seized upon.

But this brings us back to the incompleteness of Scots as a language and to a third basic question: how far can poetry avoid the law of diminishing returns if it tries to survive in a language/dialect which is not at the same time used for all other forms of communication such as in newspapers, schools, churches, business? In this connection it is interesting to note how the editorial policy of *Gairm* recognises this danger and so encourages the use of Gaelic over a wide spectrum of purposes. Significantly there is no such consistent endeavour on behalf of Scots.[1] Exactly what form such an endeavour could take is hardly clear. The most sanguine, as well as one of the least polemical, expressions of such possibilities, came recently from Edwin Morgan: "I think that Scots could be revived. That's what the Israelis have done with Hebrew, deliberately revived it as an act of national policy, and it has worked; something like this could happen with Scots. This really depends upon the political situation; I don't think you can start, as Hugh MacDiarmid wanted to do, from using Scots and then move from that into politics. I think that the politics have got to happen and then you decide what language you are going to have in a new, independent Scotland."[2] This is sanguine not only in its skating over of the crucial and obvious differences between the situation of Hebrew and that of Scots but also in its willingness to contemplate political developments of such depth and magnitude as to call forth a broad-based desire on the part of the Scottish people to extend, deliberately, the everyday use of Lowland Scots. Similar arguments have of course been put forward for Gaelic. (But what happens along the Highland Line, north of which Lowland Scots may be more foreign than English and south of which Gaelic will be more foreign still?) But it is surely right to stress the communal basis of the language a poet draws upon: a substantial and significant body of poetry in Scots (or Gaelic) would not develop unless the majority of the population were to speak, read, think and feel in Scots (or Gaelic).

It is clear then that any discussion of English/Scots/Gaelic poetry simply in terms of what language it is in will be severely limited. The viewpoint must include the more basic considerations of how far a particular writer's response to a particular tradition limits him to a rearguard action, and how far it allows him or impels him to extend the tradition in such a way that his poetry may take a significant place *vis a vis* both contemporary life in Scotland and contemporary life and literature outside Scotland. It cannot expect any special critical allowances.

* * *

MacDiarmid's attempt to revive Scots for literary purposes began half a century ago and is outside our present scope, but it is worth recalling briefly the feelings and ambitions associated with

155

the attempt. In his *Chapbook* for February 1923 he declared: "We have been enormously struck by the resemblance—the moral resemblance—between Jamieson's *Etymological Dictionary of the Scottish Language* and James Joyce's *Ulysses*. A *vis comica* that has not yet been liberated lies bound by desuetude and misappreciation in the recesses of the Doric: and its potential uprising would be no less prodigious, uncontrollable, and utterly at variance with conventional morality than was James Joyce's tremendous outpouring." A month later he described the vernacular as "a vast unutilised mass of *lapsed observation* made by minds whose attitudes to experience and whose speculative and imaginative tendencies were quite different from any possible to Englishmen and Anglicised Scots today." Looking back on this in a broadcast (24/1/54) he recalled: "The very first poem I wrote straight from the dictionary, when it occurred to me—an experience almost like that of religious conversion —that my opposition was not to the Scots language but to the kind of stuff I feared most writers would employ it for if its use were revived, was "The Watergaw," which showed me conclusively that I could write much better lyrical poetry in Scots than I'd ever been able to do in English."[3]

That extraordinary phrase "straight from the dictionary" is in one sense literally true: his early knowledge of and feeling for such Scots as he grew up with was, when he came to use it for poetry, reinforced by direct recourse to lexicographers, especially Jamieson. In some cases the evidence is raw, where we find clusters of alliterating words picked from the same few pages of the dictionary; and since he drew words from widely differing areas and periods the over-all result bears little resemblance to any language spoken by men. But what attracted him, like the glitter that attracts a magpie, was the power of certain Scots words to discriminate and particularise in a manner he felt lacking in any possible English equivalents. As any comparison between his early English and his early Scots lyrics will show, the access of clarity and power were startling.[4] He was also able to achieve a greater lyrical compression through the use of Scots words which have a wider range of connotation than any single English alternative. In

> Earth's littered wi' larochs o' Empires,
> Muckle nations are dust . . .

"larochs" suggest not just ruins as such but also ruins of a humble kind (cottages, barns) and "muckle" implies a degree of familiarity over and above simple notions of size. And if we take a familiar verse like this:

> I' the how-dumb-deid o' the cauld hairst nicht
> The warl' like an eemis stane
> Wags i' the lift;
> An' my eerie memories fa'
>   Like a yowdendrift.

If we take this and transliterate it into English we can see the extent to which it particularises a mode of consciousness which belongs absolutely to that form of expression.

> In the still dead centre of the cold harvest night
> The world like a teetering stone
> Sways in the sky;
> And my eerie memories fall
>   Like a swirling drift of snow.

Translation in any meaningful sense seems to be out of the question, at least into English.

In the vivid hallucinatory perspectives of the Scots lyrics, and then in the meditative coiling and uncoiling of *The Drunk Man Looks at the Thistle*,[5] MacDiarmid's individual achievement was totally at odds with any historical expectations which may have been entertained about the lack of prospects for the use of Scots. But there was a further dimension: paradoxically, this individual and even idiosyncratic achievement was presented as an item in a prolonged and vociferous programme for the general revival and resuscitation of Scots. How much width of interest this generated is difficult to say.[6] And any followers who wished to implement the programme, as poets, were faced with a dilemma: they had access to the same linguistic sources as MacDiarmid used but what they did not have access to was an equally powerful individual vision. In weaker hands the tactics adopted by MacDiarmid towards the resources of Scots were self-defeating: for instance the typical model would be not the inimitable mode of the lyrics (although there were attempts to imitate them) but rather the dense virtuosic performance of "Water Music," i.e. skilful word-play with the help of a dictionary

157

or two. This does not of course exclude different tactics, but if we consider such poetry as can be directly related to MacDiarmid's Scots as a primary influence, we cannot, despite opinion to the contrary, find much of lasting significance.[7]

MacDiarmid's influence, both benevolent and malevolent, is considerable and will remain so. Its principal force however will arise from his basic questioning, not so much in theory as in his practice, of just how poetry can react to and accommodate the proliferating information and the direct political concerns of contemporary life. There is no point in trying to measure his influence in terms of how many people are writing or not writing verse in Scots. Nevertheless his unique achievement is there, a rock face dominating a landscape, and any poet who does commit himself to the resources of Scots must, explicitly or implicitly, work out his own orientation to that achievement.

*　*　*

If we may step aside briefly from the specific question of Scots, an interesting parallel may be drawn with Sorley Maclean, whose acceptance and resuscitation, in highly individual terms, of his own Gaelic tradition represents a unique achievement no less remarkable than MacDiarmid's within the Scots tradition. And if we are thinking of non-English traditions then the Gaelic one is every bit as much a part of the Scottish heritage as the Lowland Scots one (more so, partisans would claim). At any rate, such a reference adds a useful dimension behind or beyond the immediate subject.

The bulk of Maclean's most important work belongs to the late thirties and early forties and has been familiar to his Gaelic readers since then: but it is interesting to see how a wider attention to his work and its background arose in the late sixties and early seventies.[8] Drawing on rhetorical procedures which meant little or nothing to current English poets, and on a sense of loyalty to family ramifications (as evident recently in his "Elegy to Calum I. Maclean" of 1968) which could appear anachronistic in a shifting urban society, Maclean created, with a little help from other sources such as Donne and Yeats, a mode of encountering his contemporary world head-on. The personal element was crucial, for the crisis that forced his best poetry into existence arose from the combination of a personal affair and an agonised response to the situation in Europe created by the Spanish Civil War. These two strands coalesce and pull apart with a strength of passion and hard intellect that gives his poetry, despite the veils of translation and the passage of thirty years, a present voice:

> I cannot worship or extol
> Nature which made my intellect whole,
> the single mind and the divided soul. (*Eimhir*, XVIII)

Thus we are tugged from one pole—

> I've built you a tall monument
> on the crumpling mountains of our time,
> yet this is a memorial
> that men will speak of when you're dumb
> and though I lose you, and another
> enjoy you to his every wish
> you'll blaze and glitter in my songs
> after the setting of your flesh. (XIX)

—to the other:

> Let me lop from my verse every grace
> shed by the lustre of your face,
> and let it learn the economy
> of Liebknecht's death and slavery:
> let me burn away each leaf
> that grew joyfully from my grief.
> And let me hammer the people's wrongs
> into the iron of my songs. (XXXII)

In other poems, like the long "The Woods of Raasay" (1940) and "Hallaig" (1954)[9] we can see the precisely mapped local particulars acting as growth and anchor points for a clarity of vision which can only be described as mystical, registering influences from deep in the subconscious.

To those outwith Gaeldom (most of us) the judgment of critical responses is of course difficult. To those within, there is no doubt whatever of Maclean's major status. In the following paragraph by Iain Crichton Smith, for instance, we find a characteristic combination of a recognition of Maclean's achievement and a recognition of the odds against which it occurred: "It seems to me that here in process of formation we have a new kind of Highland consciousness, brought to the complexities and dialectic of history, and immersing itself in their element. It is astonishing that a Highlander brought up in such a narrow world (though broadened by a liberal education at Edinburgh University) should not have succumbed in the furnace of Communist ideology, a love affair of great intensity, and a cause demanding decision of poets and artists. It is precisely this creative confusion which produced the poetry: one feels that no other combination of factors would have been enough. It produced a union of the sophisticated and the primitive, of the intelligence and the passions, which is quite unique in Gaelic literature. It probably will not happen again in the conceivable future. That it should have happened at all seems little short of miraculous."[10]

The awareness of belonging to a dying language is an inevitable part of Gaelic consciousness—

> I cannot see the sense
> of writing in a dying tongue
> now that Europe, raped and torn,
> moans behind my song . . . (LV)

—yet, despite routine and rather unrealistic attempts to draw parallels with Czech, Hebrew and Romansch, there does persist a feeling that an enclave of Gaelic can be preserved in the Hebrides. When asked if he accepted this possibility Maclean replied: "Yes, against the day, a sort of remnant against the better day. Oh yes, I think so."[11]

Clearly Maclean's work has been important for other Gaelic poets, though among George Campbell Hay, Derick Thomson, Iain Crichton Smith and Donald MacAulay, it is Smith who shows the clearest signs of influence. Since Maclean's work was not presented, as was MacDiarmid's, as part of a platform, the question has not been bedevilled by polemics. Just what kind of development is feasible in either case is anyone's guess. For several years now practical steps have been taken to try to save Gaelic, but without any reasonable prospect of maintaining the necessary reserve of monoglot speakers it is hard to escape the impression of stable doors being closed after the horse has fled; though an interesting

160

corollary to the dwindling of native use is the increase of Gaelic learning on the part of outsiders. Yet despite contemporary inadequacies, evidenced in English loan-words, Gaelic is at least a complete language in a way in which Scots is not. People at least recognise what they are fighting for, whereas there is little general agreement (even among its most avid supporters) as to what exactly the "Scots language" is, who speaks it and on what occasions. It is possible that because of its incompleteness and its closeness to English, the resources of Scots will remain open to poetry for longer. The epitaphs so far composed for both have proved premature.

* * *

Of the poets writing in Scots today I would suggest that Robert Garioch is the most significant in terms of an acceptance of a tradition (linguistic and literary) and a utilisation of that tradition as a mode of formulating a personal and readily communicated response to certain pressures that impinge upon the individual. His committal to the use of Scots is positive and lifelong and any signs of direct and specific indebtedness to MacDiarmid's work in Scots are of limited importance: it is certainly unfair to label him a "MacDiarmid Makar"—a phrase reminiscent of the patronising "Scottish Chaucerian" now happily defunct.

Obvious points of contrast with elements of MacDiarmid do suggest themselves as pointers to a general description. David Black has sketched differences in poetic persona in this way: "on the one hand we have a personality essentially *social*: informal, humorous, entertaining, melancholy, closely and affectionately observant of human rituals and absurdities; on the other a man always separate, alone with a peculiar and intense vision of the cosmos, or alone lecturing passionately from a high platform—benevolent also, no doubt, but with the self-proclamatory 'love' of the evangelist or the politician, rather than with the happy tolerance of the friend." The thematic recurrences in Garioch show "a continuity of person-ality, not, as in the case of the thematic recurrences in MacDiarmid's work, a continuity of message." In Garioch "the poem is written *for* the reader, so to speak: it recognises his equal and personal humanity; whereas with MacDiarmid the poetry is written more purely *from* the poet, and the readers look on, involving themselves

161

where they can."[12] Roderick Watson has added that Garioch's work "contains the humility which pertains to a man who knows his craft thoroughly and has few pretensions beyond it—*pace* MacDiarmid and his uncanny *Weltanschauung*."[13]

Within his range the achievement is considerable and it reaches much further than the celebration of humane and genial virtues. Certainly these virtues are immediately recognisable in the comic aspects of his work, but it contains also an astringent, at times even a bleak element and it is here that the deepest roots of his poetry lie. However our picture will be equally distorted if we insist, as one reviewer recently did, that that grim vision represents the "real" Garioch and that otherwise he is hiding behind comic procedures or other men's clothes (i.e. translation).[14] The gradations and the ambivalencies between the comic and the baleful do not support clear-cut divisions of this kind. And his translations surely represent something more positive than escapism. In the first place, his response to the technical challenge of translating from such variegated sources as Pindar, the Anglo-Saxon, George Buchanan's Latin, Schiller, Goethe, Guiseppe Belli's Romanesco and Apollinaire, is what one would expect from one of the most skilled craftsmen writing in Britain today in any language. Further, in his role as makar it is natural that his translations should indicate an attitude of equality and freemasonry with fellow-makars, especially if, as with Belli, there seems to be a temperamental affinity, without this in any way impeding the openness of his fellowship with lay audience or reader.

Without suggesting a model as crude as a straight line through from the genial to the desperate it is still possible to indicate samples or groupings of poems which take us through these recognisably distinct areas: (i) poems of comic satire (ii) poems of a more serious and awkward questioning (iii) poems of dilemma and entrapment.

The Edinburgh Sonnet "Did Ye See Me?"[15] is familiar to those who know Garioch's work but for others it is a useful starting point and illustrates the features of the first group.

> I'll tell ye of ane great occasioun:
> I tuke pairt in a graund receptioun.
> Ye cannae hae the least perceptioun
> hou pleased I was to get the invitatioun

162

tae assist at ane dedicatioun.
And richtlie sae; frae its inceptioun
the hale ploy was my ain conceptioun;
I was asked to gie a dissertatioun.

The functioun was held in the aipen air,
a peety, that; the keelies of the toun,
a toozie lot, gat word of the affair.

We cudnae stop it: they jist gaithert roun
to mak sarcastic cracks and grin and stare.
I wisht I hadnae worn my M.A. goun.

The poem requires little comment. The solid rhyming in the octet ridicules the old Scots "-ioun" abstract suffix and this is neatly linked to the sestet in "functioun" and toun/roun/goun. Again the scorn evinced in the sestet is but the exposure of the situation established in the octet: the speech was made, after all, at the speaker's own invitation. It is worth adding that the M.A. gown has been (and may still be) a revered article in Scottish society. The barbs here are directed towards the narrator. In "Elegy"[16] they are released, against the subjects of the elegy, in a delayed action made possible by the use of the sonnet-form. "They are lang deid," the poem begins and throughout the octet we accept the implications of the title. The "firm-set lips" and "sherp-tempert een" of the headmasters do not necessarily disturb us, and we are assured that they were "wycelike, bienlie men." However the very last word of the octet has an acidic touch—the poet, the "new cleckit dominie" found himself in "their den." The sestet drops the elegiac pretence altogether while the last line, snatching out like a vicious hook, ensures there is no escape. Elegy is revenge, even if it is premature.

Ane tellt me it was time I learnt to write—
round-haund, he meant—and saw about my hair:
I mind of him, beld-heidit, wi a kyte.

Ane sneerit quarterly—I cudna square
my savings bank—and sniftert in his spite.
Weill, gin they arena deid, it's time they were.

163

piled on the soil" but has also associations of prestige, wealth (albeit of a former age) and solidity: "Regency wark," with "stane-aircht cellars" and "weill-jyned flagstanes." So the worm that enters the poet's "deeded stane-and-lime property" brings pre-monitions of the natural subterranean life at work underneath the mass of civilised stone. Yet the disturbance of his security and composure is minimal and he remains the jocose owner-occupier engaged in keeping his property respectably clean.

> I was abaysit wi thochts of what was gaun-on ablow my feet,
> that the feued and rented grund was the soil of the naitural
> Drumsheuch Forest,
> and that life gaed on thair in yon soil, and had sent out a spy,
> thinkan some Friend of the Worms had slockent them wi a shoure,
> whan I on my side of the crust had teemit twa-three pails of water,
> meaning to scrub the place doun wi a besom I had jist bocht . . .

Such gentle contemplation of the wonders of nature are indeed possible *because* of his security.

> I watched, and thocht lang of the ferlies of Naitur; I didna muve;
> I thocht of the deeps of the soil, deeper nor the sea . . .

But the second encounter, over in a flash, disrupts everything and as the poem snaps shut, a new and horrifying dimension of nature snaps open:

> A rat raxt frae a crack atween twa stanes.
> I shuik wi sudden grue. He leukit at me, and wes gane.

The agreeable pact between man and worm is shattered. Between man and rat there is fear on both sides and on the man's part disgust as well.

A different and more ambiguous encounter is described in "My Faither Sees Me."[21] The poet, busy about his affairs in a secure routine, catches sight of his reflection in a darkened window—but it is not his own image that catches him unawares:

> My faither sees me throu the gless;
> why is he out there in the mirk?
> His luik gaes through me like a dirk,
> and mine throu his, baith merciless.

166

This endless muir is thrang wi folk
that hirple aye aa airts at aince
wi neither purport nor content
nor rest, in fidgan impotence.

The most active prisoners try to penetrate the wire but are immediately
shot down then devoured by dogs. Yet where they fall their blood
fertilises the bare earth and up come gaudy flowers which "begowk
the man that nourished them." Others tether themselves so that
they are confined to safe areas—these are either wiser than the
rest or more easily terrified by the wire. Yet the ground where they
stay is barren, unwatered by blood. Caught in this dilemma between
bloody sacrifice and sterile survival a third group, "slaw-gaun folk,"
shrink in upon themselves:

And aye alane or twae by twae
they gang unhurt amang the noy
of thon fell planet, and their een
lowe wi the licht of inward joy.

But this minimal existence is barren too—"Expressed in terms of
happiness/are premises of pure despair." The poem as a whole is
restricted by the determinative nature of its allegorical point, and
formally its four-square quatrains (forty of them) tend to impede
the kind of development which is better served by longer lines and
fuller paragraphs, such as in "The Big Music" or "The Muir."
Nevertheless, "The Wire" does confirm very directly some of the
concerns we have already seen in some of the shorter more successful
poems.

The limitations of "The Wire" are overcome in "The Muir,"[29]
a meditative poem of 511 lines. The moor, like a highland version
of the fair field of medieval allegory, is the solid and tangible founda-
tion of the world we know through close experience.

A plewman warslin in a warld of glaur
som weit back-end, hoast-hoastin throu the haar,
kens something of the stuff that maks our warld
and plouters owre it, cursing . . .

The ploughman may accept this world as he sees it (to him the
stones are "naething but a feck of stanes"), but the poet's own

171

efforts to come to grips with it confront him with forces which in a literal sense he cannot handle:

> I grope about a boulder on the scree
> and grup it wi baith haunds and feel the strain
> endlang my airms, lift it to my thie
> and haud it, pechin, fechtin wi the pain
> that stounds my unyaised sinnons, tho I hain
> their virr by power of will, till suddenly
> the Yird's attraction on the muckle stane
> owregaes my muscles and they mutiny;
> doun faas the stane by force of gravity
> and dunsches sidelins on my muckle tae,
> shougles and comes to rest, as tho to say,
> "Ye seelie man, tak tent what ye're about."

In contrast to the sheer intractability of our physical environment, as it seems in relation to our frail bodily powers, our new knowledge of the nature of matter gives us an alarming and vertiginous sense of insecurity. Particles, for instance, obey "naething sae couthy as Newtonian laws," and the more we discover about their behaviour "the mair unsib appear effect and cause." So, our dilemma is:

> what can we dae to keep som mense
> of structure in our slidder present tense?

The new nightmare takes its place alongside the old ones, like Dante's hell ("real eneuch to him"); or the melancholia of mad Fergusson, the howl that denies our maximum powers of articulation and eloquence—

> and the mair refined,
> artistic, intellectual and nice,
> perspicuous and sedulously blind
> a man may be, the thinner is the ice . . .

—or the vision of life as service under the Grand Old Duke (of York), where both continued service *and* desertion are ignominious.

Although the world presented has "a dour/pedal note, in fremmit key, sweet-sour in tone," the one constant is our inescapable human dimensions, the only scale which gives any meaning to ideas of hell—

172

. . . our conception of the Yird itsel
is like a tree kept growan wi nae root,
nae less absurd than fire that winna quell

or ideas of heaven—

Badenoch in simmer, wi nae clegs about.

*   *   *

I have singled out Garioch's work as a centre of interest because
its *contemporaneity* distinguishes it from the vast bulk of the Scots
writing which has been alleged to constitute the Scots Renaissance.
A valid poetic response to the age in which one lives is hardly to be
engineered by the simple resort to contemporary references, just as
far-flung allusions may not obscure a basically narrow-minded
provincialism; and both of these features characterise much of the
poetry written in Scots over the past three decades. Garioch's
"Sisyphus," on the other hand, for all its use of traditional material,
could have been written in no other age than the present. Naturally,
there are elements in the tradition which he does not or cannot
utilise and I would like now to indicate some of these with illustra-
tions from other Scots-writing poets.

There is the simple lyric, for instance, a dangerous hit-or-miss
kind of poetry with, in Scots, only too many familiar resonances
to avoid. It is here that we find the best of Sydney Goodsir Smith,
in such pieces as "Saagin"—

A demon bydes in the breist in dern,
In the unkent airt
That's neither saul nor mynd nor hert;
And, whiles, like a bairn

Warslan to be born,
Hauds the haill man tense,
His genie struck in the suspense
O' onwyte, dumb at his tide's turn.

Like a globe swings throu equinox
And for a moment spins
Atween twa suns,
Nou in saagin my weird rocks.

173

or "A Tink in Reekie"—

My lass and I in the lamplicht street—
A smirr o snaw on the wind
And she smiled as the ice took her
Lauchan up in my face a tinker lass
As we left the randie howff
Bleezan ahint us.

Doomed we were and kent the haill o't—
We that were content wi luve
That ne'er wad ken content
Nor e'er forget
The nicht when mercie drouned
Incontinent.

She was a silent queyne
And she likit the cauld kiss
O' the snaw scuffan her face
As we turnit the corner then
—Ae nicht in Reekie's winter
When luve deed wi's.[30]

Smith wins through to this sharply-focussed sparseness in spite of
himself, for the general direction of his work tends towards prolixity
and posturing. It is difficult indeed to understand the high estimates
placed on his work by some of its admirers[31]—as indeed it is
difficult to understand what critical principles guided the valuations
associated with the renaissance myth in its second and third generations. Apart from the few successful lyrics, several amiable conversational performances (with neat antiphonies of bookish and colloquial
manners),[32] and some adept translation,[33] the bulk of Smith's
work is vitiated by glib patriotism and a ready resort to faded
rhetorical cast-offs.

Smith was born (1915) in New Zealand, of Scottish family, and
went through the English public school system: his adoption of
Scottish residence and letters was thus by deliberate choice. Poetically, this patriotism-by-conversion led him to ride rough-shod over
simple historical facts—as when in a poem written in 1942 on the
Nazi oppression of Poland he declared

174

We ken fine the track o yon fell Rider;
Flodden and Culloden tell their tale . . .

Such a sensibility is on a par with that which in one of the love elegies uses a reference to Hiroshima as a rhetorical prop:

And weill I ken that this fey exstacie
Is nocht but Luve's Hiroshima. [34]

The poet's role, flaunted insistently, is that of Incorrigible but Lovable Wastrel, kinship being claimed with the popular romantic images of Pushkin, Byron, Burns, *et al*, just as in so many of the love-poems we find a total reliance on parallels with the stock figures of amatory history, Cuchulainn, Aeneas, Tristram, *et al*.

I, luve-doitit bard o the Westren Warld,
    That saw but coudna win
The Fortunate Isles ayont the Westren Sun
    Forge this last testament to stand
Heroic wi the tale o Helen, Cleopatra, Lesbia.
    Wi Morfydd, Dido, Heloise,
    And Mary o the whitest blee,
As Rab his Mary, Hugh his Jean,
    Sae I nou sing o three,
My ain Perdita, Phryne, Cynthia. [35]

He will undercut his rhetorical gestures with interjections like "And muckle mair i the like strain/Wi the whilk I winna deave ye nou" or "Rhetoric!/Juist sheer damned/Rhetoric!" [36] but such demurring is simply another form of sheer damned rhetoric.

Forbye theres ither subjecks for a makar's pen
    Maist wechtie and profound indeed
Maitters of war and peace and dour debate
O' foreign levie and domestic malice
    As the preachers say
        —But no for me! [37]

One only needs to think of Sorley Maclean, whose resolute refusal to consider such a denial gives his love-poetry such strength, to see how far Smith has fallen victim to the negative aspects of the tradition he adopted.

175

Another aspect of the tradition can be seen in the work of Tom Scott (b. 1918)—the weighty, didactic, socially-orientated poetry of the Poet as Preacher. The Poet as Wastrel may be an outcast because he flaunts conventional habits of decency, tidiness, canniness; the Poet as Preacher may also be an outcast, but because the people at large have not the good sense to listen to him. In such poetry there is no room for self-doubt, fine distinctions or ambiguous tensions: the purpose is confined to blunt statement, and while this can give a vigorous forward drive to the verse, from page to page, the dangers of over-simplification and *mere* moralising are obvious. "At the Shrine o the Unkent Sodger"[38] may be subtitled "A Poem for recitation" but "recitation" sounds too restrained for the loud voice and the black-and-white view of society which the piece demands. "The Ship"[39] is an uncomfortable allegory in which the Titanic is treated as a figure for the sorry culmination of European civilisation. The simplicity of the moralising and the accompanying polemical vigour of the verse, can be seen in such lines as these—

> In sicna warld the Ship cam till completion:
> Aa real values tint in ostentation.
> Food was brunt to keep the prices up
> While famine wastit millions o the fowk.
> Gowt and rickets were a twin disease
> Rackt the dividit bodie o mankind.
> Countries dee'd at some financier's whim:
> "Economie" threw faimilies in the street,
> And "policie" pit millions out o darg.
> War becam a politeecian's game
> For thinnin out the numbers o the fowk
> And findin mercats for the grub and gear
> It didnae pey sae weel to sell at hame.
> The "times" indeed were fairly out o jynt,
> But syne the "times" aye were, aye are, aye will be,
> At least until mankind has larnt to see
> The human race as yae communitie.

Certain themes of freedom and destiny are more interestingly explored in a central group of poems in the same collection. Here the implications are made clear but not distorted into over-statement: Ahab survives Moby Dick's plunge and when they surface he kills the beast and is free; Orpheus' voice survives his dismemberment and magically reassembles his body so that he now sings a new song; Telemakhos, having helped his returned father slay the suitors, realises that he himself belongs more to the suitors than to the avenging stranger; Ulysses himself, in a modern Ithaka, hungers to sail in the dark; and Adam accepts his exclusion from Eden and the necessity of finding what peace he can in being human.

And in "Brand the Builder"[40] we can see the evocation of a particular level of society at a particular time achieved through an exact focussing on details:

> Stoupan throu the anvil pend
> Gaes Brand,
> And owre the coort wi the twa-three partan creels,
> The birss air fu
> o the smell o the sea, and fish, and meltit glue,
> Draws up at his door, and syne,
> Hawkan his craig afore he gangs in ben,
> Gies a bit scrape at the grater wi his heels.
>
> The kail-pat on the hob is hotteran fu
> o the usual hash o Irish stew,
> And by the grate, a red-haired bewtie frettit thin,
> His wife is kaain a spurtle round.
> He swaps his buits for his baffies but a sound.
> The twa-three bairnies ken to mak nae din
> Whan faither's in,
> And sit on creepies round about.
> Brand gies a muckle yawn, and howks his paper out.

Neither the matter of the poetry nor the reader is bullied here—a restraint which Scott seems to find difficult for in the sequel, "Brand Soliloquizes,"[41] we are back in a welter of simplistic moralising.

The role of poet as Dominie is explicitly asserted by Scott. On the language question, for instance, he has declared: ". . . it is the duty of writers to take language from the people and raise it to full literary dignity. We should lead them, not follow like sheep-dogs after sheep. I consider that writers who try to take a cue from, instead of giving it to, the people, where language is concerned, betray their duty to the people."[42] The attractiveness of the idea is not sullied by questions of what it means in practical social, educational or publishing terms. As a critic, Scott follows an equally single-minded view of the literary tradition. He is rightly aware of the European context of earlier Scottish literature yet his narrow view of modern Scottish writing seems to preclude any such context in present-day terms. "The apocalyptic vision of New Jerusalem, of a world in which worth equals value and vice versa, permeates the poetry of Henrysoun and Dunbar, the satire of Lyndsay and the Reformers, the pasquils of the anti-unionists, the work of Fergusson and Burns, the songs of "red" Clydeside, the work of MacDiarmid, and of the later generations. It is the central stream of Scottish poetry to which others are but backwaters or tributaries."[43] As an historical summary this is dubious; as a prescriptive formula, or blueprint for the present and the future, it is stifling. When the defence of a tradition becomes a rear-guard action of this kind the law of diminishing returns seems inescapable.

On the milieu of Alexander Scott's poetry George Bruce has said this: "The speech-idiom of the North-East of Scotland compels a particularly physical articulation. Thanks to those interests, Alexander Scott had a point of entry to writing in Scots which by-passed the cul-de-sac of "Scots as a language of sentiment or feeling" and linked him to the usual activities of a community which may still be the least psychologically-divided in Scotland."[44] A good illustration of what Bruce means can be seen in A. Scott's "Heart of Stone," an extended piece written for television presentation. Both the strength of this voice as it engages with its proper subject and the limitations of possible subject (after all the satire is banal) can be gathered from such lines as these:

> Gin onie debt be here, it's haudden dern,
> Happed ahin stanes that sclent the speak o siller
> Frae raw on hauchty raw o terraced houses,
> Their snawie fronts as clean as a banker's credit
> And cauld as his arctic hert, a cranreuch beauty
> Born frae the frore skinkle o iceberg stane,
> The rock itsel (far mair nor the men that wrocht it),
> The rock steekan its ain sterk style
> On fowk whas foremaist fancy was biggan cheap

In hame-owre stane that speired the last o siller
To howk frae a hole out-by and bike in bields,
Syne fand themsels a fowk whas granite een
Were claucht in an icy wab o granite graithing,
A cauldrife chairm they never meant to mak
But hytered on by chance, the luck o the land.[45]

Although the lack of this strength is immediately apparent in his English verse, where mere alliteration is often used to whip up an impression of the desired energy, it is not simply a question of language. Although his poems have the shape of firmly articulated messages, the messages, whether in Scots or English, say very little.

Yet they are not content to remain marginal for the frequent references to the role of the makar assert, without fulfilling, a higher significance. He assists MacDiarmid in the rescue of the drowning muse of Scottish poetry from the tempestuous waves.[46] He celebrates, or says he is celebrating, fallen war-comrades.[47] He sees a sapling sprouting from the stones of a bridge and concludes (but why?) that "Scottish poets . . . too must wrench their sustenance out of stones."[48] And in a poem addressed to Alastair Mackie (b. 1925) "and the younger Scots makars," A. Scott (b. 1920) claims that

> . . . naebody born i the north sen 1920
> Wad scrieve in aucht but Suddron (sweet and gentie).
> . . .
> While skeelie stepsons tirled the t'ither tongue
> In ilka airt (and insches gey far-flung)
> Wi aa the beuks o ballants fremmit-fou,
> Sen nane but Scotts in Scots wad "mak it new."[49]

Clearly some kind of apostolic role is envisaged.

Alastair Mackie's Scots is denser, with a tendency towards forms which *The Scottish National Dictionary* lists as less usual. His recent collection, *Clytach*,[50] with about 640 lines of verse, has a glossary of over 600 words. The very title draws attention to the alleged barbarous nature of the tongue used, for "clytach" is glossed as "barbarous speech." Three of the poems in the book are specifically about this dilemma. In "Châteaux en Ecosse" he laments the near inaccessibility of the way his grandmother talked:

179

Here's me blawin on the cauld ess o her tongue
tae bigg, châteaux en Ecosse, thae bit poems.

The self-deprecation is more comic in "Scots Pegasus," for the Scots
Pegasus is a sort of clockwork wooden horse "wi a humphy back
and cockle een"—possibly the unlikely creature could fly but
"naebody, dammt, kens the horseman's wird." More positively,
in the final poem, "Probe," he likens his position to that of a daddy
longlegs or a space module, both waiting and sensitive to incoming
messages; for days he hears nothing, but at last

my wave linth dirls wi Lallans.
I mak oot the shaky trimmles.
I get the clash o the toun.[51]

Most volumes of poetry in Scots contain a high proportion of
translation into Scots from poets of the past. There is a positive
aspect to this which I have already mentioned. But there is also a
negative and potentially malign aspect. We have here a situation
quite different from that in which contemporary poetry is translated
for contemporary readers. We have a situation in which linguistic
resources whose survival is in doubt are measured against poetry
which in its day was fresh and new. Is there any current original
writing in Scots capable of matching the vigour and inventiveness
of the Scots used by Edwin Morgan for translating Mayakovsky?
If the frontiers of linguistic testing and play are to be found in
translations from the past rather than in creation for the present,
what can be shaped for the future? When we consider this, along
with the frequent assertions of narrow and outmoded poetic roles,
as well as complaints about neglect, the possibilities for future
development along the familiar lines seem narrow indeed. Within
the Scots tradition today, the best of Garioch's work will last
because he has "made it new" in the only way that matters. Outside
the Scots tradition, but still within the over-all Scottish one, can we
imagine the sheer poetic energy of a writer like Iain Crichton Smith
being stalled by backward-looking anxieties?

Notes

1. The Lallans Society was founded in 1972 to promote the use of Scots: whether it will have more practical repercussions than previous enterprises of the kind remains to be seen.

2. *New Edinburgh Review* (August 1972), p. 14.

3. See also Duncan Glen, *Hugh MacDiarmid and the Scottish Renaissance* (Chambers, 1964), pp 73–83; and Kenneth Buthlay, *Hugh MacDiarmid* (Oliver and Boyd, 1964), pp 43–44.

4. See Buthlay, pp 27–29.

5. Now available in MacDiarmid's own reading from Claddagh Records, Dublin.

6. Edwin Muir demurred as early as 1936 in *Scott and Scotland*; see pp 11–16, 20–22, 32–35, 38, 41–43, 114–115, 177–81. As an Orkneyman Muir grew up remote from Lowland Scots; and for much of the period under discussion he lived in Europe. For brief comments on later phases of the so-called Scottish Renaissance see Walter Keir, "Post-War Poetry in Scots," *Saltire Review* No. 10 (Spring 1957), 61–64; and David Craig, "A National Literature?" *Studies in Scottish Literature*, Vol. 1, No. 3 (January 1964), 151–69. Craig is less than fair to those who do not engage his sympathies but he makes some useful points on Grassic Gibbon and MacDiarmid, on Douglas Young's Scots versions from the Gaelic of George Campbell Hay and Sorley Maclean, and on the songs of Hamish Henderson.

7. The latest of many expressions of opinion to the contrary is Alexander Scott's pamphlet *The MacDiarmid Makars 1923–1972* (Akros, 1972). The very title makes the assumption that all the poets listed and described owe their existence as poets to MacDiarmid's having written an important part of his work in Scots: but the assumption remains unexamined.

8. *L.R. 34* (September 1970); *Songs to Eimhir*, trans. I. C. Smith (Northern House, Newcastle, and Gollancz, 1971)—usefully reviewed by Derick Thomson in *S.I.R.* December 1971; *Four Points of a Saltire* (Reprographia, Edinburgh, 1970). For the background see the Sorley Maclean interview in *S.I.R.* May 1970, pp 10–16; Donald MacAulay's introduction to *L.R. 39* (Winter 1971); John MacInnes, "Death of a Language," *The Listener* 2:9:71.

9. The former is in *L.R. 34*, pp 9–14 and the latter was reprinted in *The Listener* 2:9:71, p. 292.

10. *Poems to Eimhir*, pp 14–15.

11. *S.I.R.* May 1970, p. 15.

12. *L.R. 23* (Spring 1967), pp 8–10.

13. *Akros 16* (March 1971), p. 69.

14. Douglas Gifford in *S.I.R.* December 1971, p. 38.

15. *Selected Poems* (Macdonald, Edinburgh, 1966), p. 26.

16. ibid, p. 30.

17. *Doktor Faust in Rose Street* (Lines Review Editions No. 3, 1973), p. 9. The title is from a 14th century poem "Quhen Alexander our kynge was dede." It is in *The Oxford Book of Scottish Verse* (O.U.P., 1966), p. 4.

18. *Selected Poems*, p. 28. Merulius Lacrymans is dry rot.

19. *Doktor Faust in Rose Street*, p. 15.

20. *The Big Music* (Caithness Books, Thurso, 1971), p. 39.

21. ibid, p. 13.

22. *Selected Poems*, p. 30.

23. ibid, p. 43.

24. ibid, p. 79.

25. ibid, p. 87, appended to his translation "The Humanists' Trauchles in Paris."

26. *Doktor Faust in Rose Street*, p. 13.

27. p. 42. The epigraph quotes from MacDiarmid's "The Drunk Man Looks at the Thistle," in *Collected Poems* (Macmillan, 1967), p. 64; see also MacDiarmid's "Lament for the Great Music," *Collected Poems*, pp 248–67.

28. *Selected Poems*, p. 51.

29. *The Big Music*, p. 18.

30. *So Late into the Night* (Peter Russell, London, 1952), p. 12; *Figs and Thistles* (Oliver and Boyd, 1959), p. 42.

31. Norman MacCaig, "The Poetry of Sydney Goodsir Smith," *Saltire Review* No. 1 (April 1954), 14–19; Kurt Wittig, *The Scottish Tradition in Literature* (Oliver and Boyd, 1958), pp 292–96; Thomas Crawford, "The Poetry of Sydney Goodsir Smith," *Studies in Scottish Literature*, Vol. VII, Nos 1–2 (July–October 1969), 40–59; Alexander Scott, *The MacDiarmid Makars*, pp 14–19.

32. *Under the Eildon Tree* (Serif Books, Edinburgh, 1948), pp 20–21; *Figs and Thistles*, pp 32–36.

33. *Figs and Thistles*, pp 55–67—Blok's "Twelve."

34. *The Deevil's Waltz* (Maclellan, Glasgow, 1946), p. 43; *Under the Eildon Tree*, p. 16.

35. *Under the Eildon Tree*, p. 18.

36. ibid, pp 44 and 62.

37. ibid, p. 13.

38. (Akros, Preston, 1968).

39. *The Ship and ither poems* (O.U.P., 1963).

40. *The Scottish Literary Revival*, ed. George Bruce (Collier-Macmillan, 1968), pp 99–102.

41. *Akros 15* (August 1970), pp 17–27.

42. *L.R.* *7* (January 1955), p. 33.
43. *The Penguin Book of Scottish Verse* (1970), p. 53.
44. *The MacDiarmid Makars*, p. 25.
45. *Cantrips* (Akros, 1968), pp 13–14.
46. "The Rescue," *The Latest in Elegies* (Glasgow, 1949), p. 50.
47. "Coronach," *Mouth Music* (Macdonald, Edinburgh, 1954), p. 20.
48. "The Stony Limit," *Double Agent* (Akros, 1972), p. 16.
49. "Mak it New," ibid, p. 47.
50. Akros, 1971. See Robert Garioch's review in *L.R.* *42/43*, pp 143–146.
51. ibid, pp 31, 39, 40.